Rifling Through My Drawers

Clarissa Dickson Wright found fame alongside Jennifer Paterson as one half of the much loved TV cooking partnership, *Two Fat Ladies*. Her autobiography, *Spilling the Beans*, was a *Sunday Times* number one bestseller and she is the author of many cookery books including *Clarissa's Comfort Food*, and *Potty: Clarissa's One Pot Cookbook* which is published later this year. She is also a passionate supporter of the Countryside Alliance and of rural pursuits. She lives a little in London but mostly in Scotland.

Rifling Through My Drawers

Clarissa Dickson Wright

HODDER

First published in Great Britain in 2009
by Hodder & Stoughton
An Hachette UK company

First published in paperback in 2010

1

A CIP catalogue record for this title is
available from the British Library

ISBN 978 0 340 97747 7

Printed and bound by Clays Ltd, St Ives plc

Hodder & Stoughton policy is to use papers that are natural,
renewable and recyclable products and made from wood grown in
sustainable forests. The logging and manufacturing processes are
expected to conform to the environmental regulations of the
country of origin.

Hodder & Stoughton Ltd
A division of Hodder Headline
338 Euston Road
London NW1 3BH

www.hodder.co.uk

To Marianne More Gordon, with more gratitude than she could ever imagine.

Contents

Acknowledgements

To Rowena Webb and Nicky Ross at Hodder for the commission and the restoration of the gun. To my agent Heather Holden-Brown and her assistant Elly James for their endless encouragement. To Chloe Billington for being my eyes and fingers, to Morag Lyall for her competence and patience, and to Marianne for another great title.

Picture Acknowledgements

Archant Norfolk: 2. © BBC Photo Library: 1, 3. Liverpool Daily Post and Echo Syndication: 6. 'Sonic' by Rodger McPhail, courtesy Sally Merison: 8. Mark Robinson: 4, 5. Courtesy the author: 7.

January

Snout's high, snow is nigh
Snout's low, there'll be snow

I have always thought surfing more exhausting than it was exhilarating. Not, bear in mind, because I spend my life riding the huge waves that break on Polynesian shores or in Hawaii. For me, the best I ever managed was to stand up on a board in Cornwall somewhere. However the last three months of 2007 reminded me of my few surfing experiences.

So it was with some relief that I got home for Christmas. I don't like Christmas, as any of you who've read my autobiography *Spilling the Beans* will know, largely because my father went out of his way to ruin it for us, so it holds nothing but unhappy memories. These days, however, with the community of my village and the friendship of the people around me, I have come to some sort of terms with it. I often go to midnight mass in the Catholic church in the village, which sadly these days seems to be held at half past nine, I don't understand why. When I was a child, and indeed a teenager, one of the highlights of Christmas was to go to midnight mass at a convent in Holland Park, run by a Spanish order of nursing nuns. My sister Heather called them the Nunny-Buns because they were all rather tiny and I can still remember the golden glow of the baroque altar and the sweet, clear, high voices of the nuns singing the hymns in Latin. We would then go into the main convent room and stand around having little cakes and eats until finally a very small and select band of us were taken into a back room, where the nuns got out their guitars and sang and danced and we would totter home, replete with sherry and sweet cakes and halva, probably somewhere around half past two in the morning.

Today, if I go to my own church, it's all over by ten o'clock. The great advantage of going there, however, is that I'm taken by my friends Philip and Mary Contini, who own Valvona and Crolla, the brilliant delicatessen on Leith Walk in Edinburgh. Philip has the most magnificent voice and makes recordings of Italian and Neapolitan songs and sings in festivals, which are events I make sure I always attend. Sitting behind him in church, Mary, his wife, says to me, 'You can sing, Clarissa' – I have an appallingly bad voice and can't sing in tune – 'Philip will drown you out.' And indeed I think this is probably the case.

Father McMullan, now a canon of St Mary's Cathedral in Edinburgh and splendid in a soutane with red buttons, conducts the service and gives us his Christmas message of thanks for the bottles of whisky and black socks that his parishioners give him. I used to be rather irritated by this but have now come to regard it as part of Christmas and would be sad if he failed to do it any longer.

The alternative, which I take some years, is to go to the church at the end of my village for the watch-night service which is at midnight and there are the usual hymns and carols and the rather welcome, hot, non-alcoholic drink. I walk down the village with my kith, who live in the big house, and then we walk back again, wishing each other a happy Christmas. But I was brought up as a Catholic and I really do prefer the Catholic service, despite its timing. The church in my village is magnificent. It's known as the visible church because you can see the spire of it for miles around and was originally built to attract the famous eighteenth-century preacher, Jupiter Carlisle. And he filled it week in, week out, for as long as he lived. Today, it's not quite so full and the Reverend Dick is driven to entertain the children with glove puppets, something I don't think would ever have occurred to Jupiter Carlisle.

Christmas Day is, of course, about food and food is really what I do best. These last couple of years, we've decided on beef and we all get together, the big house and myself and any visitor I may have and I cook the beef because that's one of the things I cook best in all the world. Magnificent beef, hung for eight weeks from a carefully chosen beast. The carcass has to have a good covering of fat or else you can't hang it for so long because it will go off. But hanging the meat is essential as it tenderises it, gets rid of excess moisture and gives it a far better flavour.

My own dear butcher, Colin Peat in Haddington, and my friend Jan McCourt in Cold Overton in Leicestershire both hang their Christmas beef magnificently and the resultant flavour and tenderness can be achieved in no other way. Never buy your beef in supermarkets because, with the best will in the world, and given the bulk of their turnover, they simply cannot hang their beef how it should be hung.

When I was a child we always had turkey on Christmas Day and one year my mother, in a rush, instead of measuring out the brandy for the brandy butter, thrust a bottle at our brilliant cook Louise as we all went rushing off to the hospital for my father to do the rounds and be home in time to carve the turkey. When we got back in time for a late Christmas lunch I went into the kitchen and there sitting beside an uncooked turkey was Louise, merrily waving the remains of a brandy bottle and singing Christmas carols and such songs as 'White Christmas' to the turkey. I don't remember what we had for lunch that day but if it was the turkey, we must have had to cut it up for ragout.

Anyway, at the end of the year I felt exhausted. *Spilling the Beans* had been published in September and I had said to Kerry Hood, the Pollyanna publicist with the steel spine who I was privileged to have from my publisher, 'Work me to death, kill me, it doesn't matter, just so long as it's a success.' Sadly she took me literally. Had I known the book was going to go straight to number one on the bestseller list, I would probably have stayed home by my fire and toasted my toes. As it was, I spent the rest of the year visiting various literary festivals over and above my usual workload of speaking engagements.

I have never been a fan of literary festivals, which seem to me to be an exploitation of authors, since you sell a limited number of books and the main profit goes to the organisers, although it's enjoyable meeting the people who turn up. This wouldn't be so bad if the festivals were aimed at the sort of authors who really need the exposure and the publicity, but this is not the case because what every festival seeks are the big names that draw in the crowds. The only possible exception to this is Clare Throckmorton at the Throckmorton Literary Festival, who believes that even unknown authors should be given a chance.

Kate Adie threw a different perspective on literary festivals for me. She was one of the joys of this particular tour (Kate does a lot of literary festivals and I have often wondered why), and when I found myself on a platform with her at Cheltenham talking about political correctness she said that in this day and age when there were so few forums where people could meet and discuss issues, she felt that the literary festival provided one such. On consideration, there is actually quite a lot to say for that point of view.

So maybe Kate Adie is right, as she so often is. It was quite fascinating talking to her about the present system of news coverage which rather prevents active journalists in the field going out to discover what is happening for themselves because they have to be back to appear in front of a television camera, every hour on the hour for twenty-four-hour news. I particularly love the reason why she always wears pearl earrings. Apparently when she was first a daring journalist going into dangerous places, the dreaded Roy Hattersley said that he hated to think of her hampering the troops and holding them up while she stopped to look for a pearl earring. At that point, as I understand it, she had never worn pearl earrings, but she has never failed to wear them since. That is the sort of humour I really enjoy. Roy Hattersley, you may remember, was the columnist who wrote in the *Evening Standard* when *Two Fat Ladies* started: 'These two women will never succeed.' Wrong again there, Roy! And a pity you couldn't control your dog to stop it killing geese in St James's Park.

Anyway, gentle readers, please don't misunderstand me. I greatly enjoyed meeting all of you who came to hear me at the various festivals and listening to your news and problems. I was particularly interested by the number of people who appeared from my past or indeed from my family's past, whose existence I hadn't even known about. And undoubtedly one of the great highlights of those months was the number of people who either wrote to me, or came and spoke to me and told me that they had been helped by what I had written about my own alcoholism and that they had come into recovery or had joined Alcoholics Anonymous because of it. That was, I suppose, more important to me than anything else, and I delighted in it.

My final speech was in Ely and, rather wonderfully, the only place large enough for the number of tickets they'd sold was Ely Cathedral, so that I found myself giving my talk under the octagon of that beautiful, magnificent cathedral. Step five of AA says that you share your step four, your inventory, which I suppose is what *Spilling the Beans* was, with God and another human being and I certainly felt when I was sitting under the octagon that God was very much in the equation.

We have the great dichotomy in this country between Christmas, the birth of the Christ child, who brings hope and light to the world, and Yule, the ancient, pagan winter festival which, if anything, was an even greater act of faith, because halfway through the darkest part of the year they ate a sizeable amount of their stored comestibles, which gave them the necessary adrenalin rush, sugar rush and mid-winter high to avoid depression. But it also endorsed their belief that the sun would return, that spring would come, that the crops would grow and that the animals would breed again. For a primitive and early people, I think that was a huge act of faith.

At home, what I like to do best at this time of year is sleep. And then, come the Epiphany, the feast of the three kings, I can pull myself together and start whatever work I have to do for the coming year. Three Kings Night, which we don't really celebrate here, is a huge occasion on the Continent. I always used to have a spiffin' Epiphany party and then everybody could help dismantle the Christmas tree and take down the Christmas cards with me. But the best Epiphany I remember was the first time we stayed with friends in the village of Weiler, in the Lurchental in Switzerland. During the war my parents had rented a cottage from the Greenwell family who owned large parts of West Sussex around Billingshurst. One of their sons, Eddie, had come to my father during the war, having lain around being a virtual invalid as a youth, and said, 'Please could you give me a check-up because I want to join the air force?' and 'I rather lied to my doctor over the years to get out of school . . .' and things like that. So my father checked him out and found that he was perfectly healthy.

Eddie went into the Fleet Air Arm and had a heroic war, and then became a fighter pilot for Hawker Siddley. Finally, when he came into his inheritance, he bought a large part of the village of Weiler, intending to turn it into a ski resort, but he liked it so much the way it was that he just put in a couple of ski lifts and kept it very small. It was terrifically good skiing and great fun.

Their Three Kings Night was an almost pagan festival. The dwarfs who accompanied the kings on horseback around the three villages in the valley wore these amazingly carved ferocious masks which really belonged in a museum, as did the costumes that the three kings wore. They stopped at every house and accepted a glass of wine and made a mark of the cross on the door jamb to show that they had been there. As they went higher up the valley and as the drink and cold air took effect, these priceless costumes fell into snowdrifts, were hauled out, dusted down, put back on the horse and off they went again. It was all very jolly as we trooped along behind, and I loved it. We went on several occasions and if you ever find yourself in a Swiss mountain village where the locals play Spoof with viciousness worthy of a Swiss banker and can all sing 'Waltzing Matilda', even though they can speak only Schwitzerdütsch, you'll know that you're in the right place.

However, the early months of 2008 were not to give me any respite because dry rot struck. I live in a cottage built completely of stone except for the bathroom extension and it was in the bathroom wall that we found the dry rot just before New Year. I moved out. I had a book to write, the bath was going to have to come out, the wall was going to have to come down, the whole place was going to be sprayed with toxins in order to defeat the dry rot and a house with no bath and an unusable kitchen was no place for me to stay and write about comfort food.

Clarissa's Comfort Food should have been the easiest of books to write, made up of those tried and tested recipes that I had always enjoyed. I took myself off to the Cholmondeley Arms, my favourite pub in Cheshire, down near the Shropshire border, which is owned and run by my old friend, Carolyn Ross-Lowe. She and her late husband Guy started the pub twenty years ago and it's everything a pub should be. It's in an old school, converted so that ex-pupils come back to take a drink where they once studied, and while it isn't a gastro-pub as such, it serves excellent food, such as delicious oxtail, kedgeree, marvellous steaks and always roasts on Sunday. It sources much of its food locally from the Cholmondeley Estate, which runs a hub for produce from its various farms. The pub has a great atmosphere and is full of entertaining and amusing locals, everything from a QC to Johnnie O'Shea who hunted the Cheshires for twenty-five years, and is a whippety man, with endless stories about his training as a boy in Ireland and about his time hunting. Ginger McCain, the trainer, is also a regular and comes in with his clients.

One reads that country pubs are failing at a rate of knots and why should I doubt what I read in the newspapers? I have been to a lot of pubs that I would be quite happy to see fail: a combination of Brake Brothers food and microwaves and very little effort to make the customer feel welcome is a sure-fire sign for failure even in the best of times. Cheshire is a well-off county. Somebody once said that the occupants lived above their means in Cheshire as opposed to above their shops in Manchester and there is an element of truth in that, but basically it is a good rural farming community.

The strip of England that runs from Lancashire down to Somerset in the south is cheese and dairy country. Historically the cheese came about because there is a strain of salt that runs right through the grassland soil and the grass and flavours the milk, and perfectly complements the cheese; and there are salt mines all along that stretch which were used to help to preserve the cheese. It is a curious fact that Red Leicester cheese is now made entirely in Shropshire, because cheese-making in Leicestershire had died out and Shropshire took over the name. As a result there is a farmer in Leicestershire who by law was unable to call his delicious, genuine Red Leicester cheese by that name and had to call it Sparkenhoe. I recommend it to you. But of course the delicious cheeses of Cheshire and Cheddar and Lancashire all fall within this belt.

The biggest cheese fair in the world is held at Nantwich in Cheshire, just down the road from the Cholmondeley. If you win at Nantwich, you win in the world. I went one year to judge and was astonished at the variety. There were cheeses from every part of the universe, including China: not very nice cheese from China, but cheeses all the same. And the Artisan section, which was the one I was most interested in, had some fantastic products, especially the ones from that strip of England. The artisan producer who won that year, a Mrs Appleby, produced hand-made Cheshire cheese the likes of which make you understand why Cheshire cheese is so astonishingly popular.

The decline in the dairy industry has not affected this part of the world so much as elsewhere, largely because of the cheese industry. There's also been slight salvation thanks to the growth of coffee bars selling lattes and skinny lattes, though why you would want a skinny latte, I'm not quite sure. The rich grasslands of the area have always encouraged the dairy industry and you get full herds of dairy cattle all around the county. You come across some very curious artefacts left over from the industry in the Victorian and Edwardian eras, including walking sticks made out of bull's pizzles or penises which have a rod down the middle and a strange texture as you might imagine and are much prized among dairy farmers.

I digress. It was at the Cholmondeley that I was reunited with the motorbike and sidecar we used in *Two Fat Ladies*. This bike, which did not belong to either Jennifer or myself but was the property of the BBC, was sold for charity following Jennifer's death. The money, at my selection, went to the Butchers and Drovers Charitable Institution which is the charity for the Worshipful Company of Butchers of which I'm so proud to be a member. The bike was bought by a remarkable man called John Pointon who started his career driving a lorry for DeMolders and ended up by sheer force of hard work and determination owning the largest rendering plant in Europe. For those of you who don't know, all the bones and remnants of animals that have been butchered are burned at one or other of the country's rendering plants. This produces a great deal of power which is put back into the national grid and in the case of Pointons, they actually put water back into the River Trent, so clean is the water by the time it's been purified. John sadly died, worn out by his labours at a ridiculously young age, and his sons now run the business, so it was Martin Pointon who drove the bike over for the Cholmondeley pantomime.

Guy Ross-Lowe always used to write the pantomime for the Cheshire Hunt – and very funny they were too. It was decided to hold a fundraiser this January for the local cancer hospital that had looked after him so well in his declining days, and to stage a reprise of various sketches from the pantomimes. Guy and Carolyn's daughter Bea has the most beautiful voice and indeed has started singing professionally, so she sang the majority of the songs.

The show was called *The Wrong Pantomime* and featured characters from the previous productions, who all discovered they were in the wrong pantomime. In the finale the baddies were fighting the goodies and the baddies were winning, as so often happens in this world, and the goodies were shouting, 'Help, help, who will save us? Who will save us?' On came the *Dam Busters* music, the lights went out and there were spotlights and smoke, and through the curtains, vroom vroom, came the motorbike and sidecar with me in my Biggles helmet and we got the biggest cheer of the night. It was a great occasion. In rehearsals the chap who was driving the bike said, 'It keeps stalling!' I said, 'It's all right, it'll be all right on the night.' To which he responded, 'Clarissa, it's a motorbike, not a person.' And I said, 'Trust me, that bike is a person.' And lo and behold, I was right, it was fine on the night. It was the greatest joy to see the bike again. I do go and have a little play with it in Staffordshire whenever I'm in that part of the world. But I think it likes an audience first, that dear bike.

The year saw the twentieth anniversary of the Cholmondeley Arms and Dan Whitmore, their enthusiastic new young chef, and I cooked an anniversary dinner which took place later in the year, as you will understand since the menu was almost entirely game. The dinner sold out more or less immediately and we cooked for, I think, seventy people, which was as many as the pub would hold, all packed in. Hugo Thompson, the extremely handsome manager who brings in the young, had the idea and the event made the local papers and was a splendid celebration. I like getting into the kitchen and getting my hands dirty and watching chefs be pleasantly surprised that I'm actually able to cook. I don't know what they think I do, but there we are.

The flat lands of Cheshire around the Cholmondeley also provide great hunting country. There is the Cheshire Hunt and the Wynnstay Hunt and the Cheshire Forest, all fairly close together. If you were driving up one of the roads, you'd come across a pub called the Blue Cap with a large hound as the pub sign. Blue Cap was the famous hound who ran a race at Epsom for some enormous amount of money, and was the great stud hound for the Cheshire Hunt. I'm not going to have my rant about hunting here; I'll talk to you about it later on.

January also saw, I think, one of the most wonderful occasions of my life, and this is a life, remember, that has been filled with pretty amazing things. The last fourteen years alone, since the start of *Two Fat Ladies*, have seen me in many remarkable places with nothing as dear to my heart as this. I had been at the Melton Mowbray Food Festival the previous autumn when a woman came up to me and asked if I would come and speak to her Women's Institute. I often give talks to the WI, since I'm an enormous fan of theirs and once described them as the SAS of cookery after they defeated Europe over the question of marmalade. Were it not for the WI, we would no longer have marmalade, we would no longer have kippers, and we would not have a great many things.

I remember the first time I spoke to them was in Worcester and I was expecting, I don't know, forty, perhaps fifty people.

When I arrived, the antis – those who campaign against hunting, animal research and all field sports – having been taken away by the police, I asked the president, 'And how many people am I speaking to?' She replied, 'Oh, we could only fit in 740.' I went in to do my talk and I looked at them, rank upon serried rank of women of all ages and I said, 'Do you know what I see? Raw power!' And they all cheered.

However, this WI was at Sandringham and they said, 'Our president will be there.' And it did not immediately strike me that the president of the Sandringham WI is Her Majesty the Queen. Now the Queen has been my Queen since I was not quite five years old and she's somebody whom I hold in the greatest respect and esteem; in a world where I have very few heroes, she is definitely one of them. When the day finally dawned, I was so excited that I was on the road from the A1 to Sandringham at half past nine in the morning. It only takes an hour and a bit at worst to get to Sandringham from there and so I spent a lot of time driving around, sitting reading my book, looking at views, until it was time to present myself. I was taken to lunch, and then to the hall. I was dreadfully overexcited, like a small child. When you meet the Queen, and I have done so before, you are amazed at how good-looking she is, how vital she is. Her skin is wonderful and glows with health, she has great hair and an enthusiasm for life which you seldom find in people who occupy great estates for a long time. We had a lovely day. She was kind enough to laugh in all the right places when I spoke, and the WI performed the most hilarious Laurel and Hardy sketch, which had us all weeping with laughter. Then we had a very good tea – as you would expect.

I said to the Queen, of one lady who'd won the baking competition and was ninety-four, that she still lived on her own and got her own tea every day, and the Queen said, 'Good heavens, how would you have the energy?' I thought, Well, there's no doubt the Queen has the energy, but she probably doesn't get her own tea much. Though I gather she cooks a mean bacon and eggs. When I drove away, I was in a little golden bubble and rang up all my friends and told them I'd been speaking to the Queen, so I thought I might as well share it with you too. And that really took me through January.

Meanwhile I could still not go home because the Scottish builders who had been employed to fix the dry rot were behaving like builders everywhere and failing to get the job done. Everybody said to me, 'Don't come home; the bath is still in the middle of the kitchen, the place smells of chemicals, so you couldn't have a bath, you couldn't cook, and you could barely get past the bath to go upstairs. Don't bother to come home.' But how I longed for my dear little home. January and February are usually the months I do spend at home, but not this year.

Salvation came in the form of a most remarkable man called Trevor Harding. Trevor is an ex-naval commander who, in his seventies, still swings from the roofs of Edinburgh, examining the tiles and all the things that go wrong with roofs on Georgian houses. He has put together a team of central European builders, mostly Polish, but the plumber is a charming young man from Latvia and he gets the job done. Sadly, by the time Trevor was found and put into my house to make right of wrong, it was too late for me, it was March and I had to get on with life.

Don't worry, I haven't forgotten February, I was just running ahead of myself. So there I was, stranded at the Cholmondeley Arms trying to write my book on comfort food, without a kitchen. Although with quite a lot of comfort and consoled by the hearty breakfasts and iconic fried bread of Shirley Collins, who runs the lodging side of the Cholmondeley, and in fact seems to run life for everybody in Cheshire; Mother Shirl, she's known as. She's very much the sort of earth mother, Ma Larkin type who nurtures me, did my washing for me and all sorts of kind things like that. But then of course, to pile Pelion on to Ossa my laptop crashed, the hard disk went, or the hard drive or whatever it's called. But fortunately in Malpas there is a firm called i7 who not only sell computers, but also deal with all the ills that seem to plague this pestilential tool of my trade, and a delightful young man called Steve not only saved the data that I hadn't saved on my hard disk – I know, don't lecture me – but also sold me for really very little money another laptop, and off I went to get it. I seemed to be running down to i7 on a fairly regular basis at that time, largely because I couldn't get to grips with the new computer, but I couldn't send anything from it as none of us had realised that it didn't have an internal modem and so I could only sit outside their premises and send the text of my new book to my publisher by wireless, until we discovered the flaw.

I don't like computers. I've written, now, fourteen books on a laptop and I'm still not terribly happy with the tool. Although I'm computer literate, I don't love it and I go on the Internet as little as possible because I distrust the information it provides. When we were filming *Clarissa and the Countryman* we were due to film at New Abbey in Dumfriesshire, perhaps better known as Sweetheart Abbey, and a BBC researcher arrived with some notes that she subsequently admitted she had got from the Internet that said 'Devorgilla, wife of John Balliol, King of Scotland', and I said, 'No, wrong.' She said, 'What do you mean?' I replied, 'She was wife of John Balliol, founder of

Balliol College, mother of John Balliol, King of Scotland. His claim to the Scottish throne came through her.' And she said, 'Well, how can you be so sure?' I looked at my books lining my sitting room and said, 'Well, where would you like to start? There are three histories of Scotland, the *Encyclopaedia Britannica* and God knows what else besides and I don't think they've all got it wrong, do you?' But had I not known this already, I dare say I would have believed her and been quite rightly pilloried by the entire Scottish nation. So don't trust the Internet. You'll blow yourself up, poison yourself or promote false information.

Tropicana Cake

This recipe for Tropicana Cake comes from the Country Markets cookbook, *A Taste of Country Markets*. Country Markets is the arm of the WI that runs the country markets and this is to remind me of the delicious pineapple fruitcake that I ate at tea with the Sandringham WI.

4oz (110g) block margarine
4½oz (125g) castor sugar
2 large eggs
4½oz (125g) self-raising flour, sieved
1oz (25g) desiccated coconut
juice and rind of 1 lemon
3½oz (100g) dried diced pineapple

Preheat the oven to 180°C /350°F/ gas mark 4.

Cream the margarine and sugar until white. Lightly whisk the eggs and gradually beat in to the margarine, followed by the flour then the coconut. Fold in the lemon rind, reserving a few strands for decoration, and the pineapple, reserving a little for decoration. Place the mixture in a 6-inch (15-cm) round cake tin, lightly oiled and lined, smoothing over the surface. Bake for 50 to 55 minutes until firm. Allow the cake to cool in the tin for 5 minutes then turn out on to a wire rack. If you like, when the cake is cold, you can mix icing sugar with enough lemon juice to make a coating consistency and ice the cake, sprinkling the remaining pineapple and zest strands over the wet icing.

February

*A blackthorn winter promises
harsh weather to come*

February is the month that the countryman hates most. Hunting is coming to an end, shooting finishes on 2 February and wildfowling slightly later. My parents were married on 2 February and my mother's brother, Vivian, who hated my father, said that it was the only gentlemanly thing that Dicky ever did, i.e. to fix his wedding for the day that shooting had ended. However, when the rest of the nation was sunk deep in gloom because there was nothing to look forward to, the weather was cold and, as Johnny Scott always said, people went on skiing holidays in February to escape the ubiquitous end-of-season pheasants, the stew that nobody really likes very much, for those of us in the coursing community February used to be a month of great excitement. Coursing is the testing of the skill and speed of two greyhounds behind a hare. Incidentally, the hare is seldom killed because it is more agile and arguably cleverer than the dog. It is also given a 100-yard start or 'law' before the greyhounds are released.

February held the two great sixty-four dog stakes, the Anglia Cup, and the Waterloo Cup at the end of the month. It is a knockout competition and, to explain it better, Wimbledon tennis tournament is based on the principles of the Waterloo Cup. The Waterloo Cup, which was the Blue Riband of coursing, was started in 1836, named not after the Battle of Waterloo, but after a hotel in Southport, whose owner persuaded Lord Sefton, a great sporting hero of the day, to hold the event at his grounds at Altcar in Lancashire. Incidentally, Lord Sefton was a great gourmet, and there are several recipes named after him which are quite delicious, the nicest being a Sefton of herring roes. Anyway, the Waterloo Cup was founded as a great coursing event and not very long afterwards the Grand National at Aintree nearby was started in order to entertain the crowds that had gathered for the Waterloo Cup. During its heyday, eight trains an hour every morning of its three days would disgorge people at a specially built station at Altcar. It was a massive sporting occasion: carrier pigeons were kept in coops to carry the result to the London Stock Exchange and to other parts of the country; Black and White whisky labels bore a picture of a black greyhound and a white greyhound turning a hare. If you have read *The Thirty-Nine Steps*, rather than watched the films, you will remember that when Mr Memory is asked who won the cup, his reply is, in this order, 'Waterloo, FA or Wimbledon?' During the 1970s the Waterloo Cup declined slightly and it was due to the efforts of racehorse trainer Sir Mark Prescott that it was resuscitated and came close to its former glories, so that by the time it was closed down in 2005 as a result of the Hunting Bill 35,000 people were accommodated in the cheap seats on the bank.

It was Johnny Scott who introduced me to the Waterloo Cup in 1995, which was the first year of *Two Fat Ladies*, and for ever after scarcely saw any of my dogs run because they were always knocked out on the Tuesday, which is the opening day, in the first round in the morning. I had usually spent the whole of that time giving interviews to journalists, explaining what coursing was about, talking to television cameras and generally trying to get people to understand this beautiful sport which had been so pilloried by the antis; huge amounts of money had been spent on advertising campaigns against it so that nobody, even people within the sporting community, really understood it. Old Lord Leverhulme, then owner of the Altcar Estate, said to me in this first year, when I complained about spending the whole morning doing these interviews, 'Are you ashamed of coursing, Clarissa?' and I said, 'No, of course not, don't be ridiculous, I love it.' And he said, 'If you believe in something and you love it then stand up for it and if you don't, don't do it.' This is a message I have carried with me, not just with coursing but with all other field sports ever since.

The Waterloo Cup is divided so that you have the nominators' (akin to stewards) car park, which is somewhat more expensive and it's rather like the enclosure at Ascot. People have picnics in the back of their cars and one wonderful man who was a captain of a lifeboat used to come across from Norfolk every year with a barrel of oysters, among other things. On the other side was the bank, a man-made hill, and this was made up of types who had come out from Southport and Liverpool and were not necessarily people you would want to meet on a dark night but we loved each other, them and me. And interspersed among them were all sorts of quite smart people, who preferred this side because you got a better view. The bookmakers were there, of course, and one of them, Steven Little, always wore his grandmother's fur coat and his father's flying boots to keep him warm because, believe me, there was nowhere colder than Altcar when the wind was coming off the Arctic.

In the morning everybody used to meet in the beer tent to get warm and drink rather good soup and have their bacon and egg butties. I remember one year when a huge man from the bank, who must have been six foot six and was wearing a singlet (at Altcar in February!), a real hard-nosed, tough guy, came up to me and whispered into my ear. What I thought he said was, 'Do you want to see my cock?' so I blushed coyly and said, 'No thank you very much. Don't you think it's rather cold and these are not the circumstances?' At which point he said, 'I've got eight of them!' He was of course talking about his running chickens, or his fighting cocks.

I have never been to a cock fight, and have no desire to go to one but this is an activity that was banned in Victorian times, not because of any cruelty to poultry, I hasten to add, but in an attempt to stop the huge amounts of money that were being gambled on such events. I know for a fact that it still exists up and down the country in various areas, which just goes to prove that if you try to ban something you simply drive it underground out of sight where it continues unregulated.

The last year of the Waterloo Cup to date, 2005, because I hope to see it restored, I decided I'd had enough of journalists, so I went to sit on the bank. On the first Tuesday morning, having told the Coursing Club that I was not available for interviews and merely intended to have a jolly time, there was a man sitting next to me who was wearing a ripped pair of rather threadbare jeans, trainers with no socks and a thin fleece. 'Good heavens,' I said to him, 'don't you have any proper clothes? You'll freeze to death out here.' And he said, 'If I'd asked for proper clothes, they might have smelled a rat.' I said, 'Whatever can you mean?' It emerged that he was on the lam from the local prison, which was an open prison, because there was no way he was going to miss what might possibly be the last Waterloo Cup. Such is the passion that it evokes in the breasts of its devotees. The bankers all said to me, 'You tell the Waterloo Cup committee, if they want to hold it next year we'll form a cordon round and we'll keep out the police.' The Waterloo Cup committee, not surprisingly, didn't accept the offer but I have no doubt that it was meant sincerely.

The other great feature, if you can put it like that, of the Waterloo Cup was the antis. Because there was a public footpath that ran through the estate, the police couldn't keep them out. In the 1970s there were quite nasty running battles between the antis and the people attending the Cup, so this time at the lunch interval the antis were allowed to march through and they stood on the footpath and hurled abuse at anybody who came anywhere near them. As this was facing the nominators' car park, this included those of us who were in it. As I reported in *Spilling the Beans*, the first year when we were filming *Clarissa and the Countryman* they stood there and yelled at me, 'One dead Fat Lady, one to go.' The BBC were quite shocked and I had to insist they filmed it because I wanted to get across quite how nasty these people were. 'Paedophiles, perverts,' they would shout, and one year a man on crutches went into the single Portaloo, which was quite near the footpath, and they attempted to push it over, with him inside it, using the poles of their banners.

The police did nothing to stop them. If I had done that, I would no doubt have been arrested for threatening words and behaviour and indeed when I used to stand by the bank and watch the antis, trying to remember their faces for other occasions, although a lot of them wore face masks or balaclavas, the police would ask me to move along because I was inciting them.

The antis were at their nastiest, however, at night in Southport, where most of us stayed, when you would be well advised to give the back alleys a wide berth. On one occasion, a group of them were chanting outside the Scarisbrick Hotel and an Irishman who'd come over for the competition said to the police, 'Why don't you move them on?' The policeman replied that they were afraid of them because the antis knew where they lived and would cause trouble at their homes. So the Irishman said, 'In that case, why don't you go away and leave us to deal with them?' To which the policeman said, 'No, we couldn't do that. They're exercising their right to protest.' And the Irishman said, 'In 1916 you shot my grandfather for exercising his right to protest.' And then, I think, moved swiftly away before he was arrested.

People were frequently beaten up in the streets. In the back of Southport, one eleven-year-old boy, son of a trainer, was grabbed by them and quite badly threatened. These are not nice people and most of them are paid to be there. I once took a journalist up to a girl who said, 'Last year I was there on the bank because it was a good way of earning £25 a day and getting to Altcar.' The journalist asked, 'Why aren't you there this year?' And she replied, 'Well, it's rather difficult with a small baby, so my brother's gone instead.'

Pamela Mason, the late widow of the actor James Mason, set up a fund simply to provide money for the antis to come to the Waterloo Cup. One year, however, they got a nasty shock. There is a rather splendid man called Vinny Faall who resigned as an RSPCA dog catcher because of the RSPCA's £5 million poster campaign against hunting and coursing, which he quite rightly said would not save the life of a single fox, deer or hare. He gave up his livelihood completely because he had no other job, and fed his family for some time on rabbits which he hunted with his lurcher. And he was on the bank one year and decided that we ought to show the antis some mettle so the whole bank marched down while the antis were on the footpath; the police gripped their batons and looked nervous, and the antis went distinctly pale as this army of huge men all in step marched along the footpath. As they came level with the antis, they broke into whistling 'Always Look on the Bright Side of Life' and marched back round again and we all cheered. It was a perfect example of the countryside's wit and pragmatic way of dealing with unpleasant situations.

Another man I very much admire for his actions is Alex Smith, a sturdy, robust Scottish socialist, who believed so firmly in coursing that he gave up his political beliefs to vote Conservative in an effort to delay the Hunting Bill.

Coursing, under National Coursing Club rules, is the perfect expression of what is a very ancient sport. If you look in the pyramids and beyond, you will see images of coursing: the Saloukis, the hounds of the Pharoahs, the Bassengis and then greyhounds, the Afghans and all the gazehounds, and dear little whippets, which were all bred specifically for coursing. During the parliamentary debate on the Hunting Bill, it seemed quite clear that various Members of Parliament could not distinguish between coursing, whose aim is not to kill the hare, and poaching, which they referred to as 'illegal coursing'. Of course there are thousands of people who hunt quite legally with their lurchers. Poaching is done at night with lamps and the betting is on the first dog to kill the hare. There is no 'law', or run-up, to the hare and when the police come along, they don't want for evidence as the corpses of the dead hares are left littering the field. This is not coursing as I know and love it, but poaching. Don't make that mistake when, as I hope it will, repeal comes.

So having had no coursing in February and still with no home, I moved on to Bath to record the unabridged edition of *Spilling the Beans* for the BBC whose audio book recording studios are there. Imagine my delight, on arriving at my hotel, to discover that among the other guests were the English rugby team. I am, as some of you may know, a huge fan of rugby. When I was a little girl my father, who was the man who turned St Mary's Hospital into a rugby hospital, used to take me to rugby matches when my mother encouraged him to do something with me. When you are four or five years old and you're sitting on the touchline, all you see are men's legs and so I'm not only devoted to rugby, I'm a great connoisseur of men's legs. I remember when I was in treatment and some poor, battered young man who'd actually been living in a skip came in and got very offended and thought I was being sexist when I told him that if he had nothing else going for him, at least he had beautiful legs. He didn't make it, sadly. He should have accepted my compliment; maybe it would have given him the self-worth he so badly lacked.

When I was living down in Sussex after I moved out of my parents' house in Circus Road, I decided to organise a rugby match between Gray's Inn rugby team and a team of my own, which I nicknamed the Dickson Rioters. We played at the back of the Yew Tree at Chalvington and Johnny Scott's father, Walter, gave us the goal posts. I even had T-shirts printed for the match which showed a Gray's Inn griffin holding a rugby ball in one hand and a pint glass in the other, which have, I believe, become collector's items. It was a great day. The Dickson Rioters were soundly thrashed, and I had sixteen people sleeping in my rather small cottage after the pig roast, which took place in the village hall in Selmeston. I remember quite a lot of people sitting on my car as I drove down the village, including the local policeman, who was perched on the bonnet, having been to the party directing the traffic.

The next day we all had to rush up to London because I had got my timing wrong and it was that great needle match between Gray's Inn and the Law Society. Hangovers don't make for good rugby and I think we lost rather disastrously that year. My junior clerk in chambers had played for the Dickson Rioters and had been greatly impressed by our fly half, nicknamed Shagger, and asked if he could borrow him to play for his team in a match in Manchester. I decided that I had better go too, to make sure that Shagger was back in London for a match the next day, so I and a man called Arthur Allen, who carried a torch for me for years and is now sadly dead, went up to the game, which took place at Salford Rugby Club, on one of the outside pitches. We had tea afterwards and I have never forgotten the delicious pickled tripe that was part of the meal – I have been trying to find the recipe ever since. Please don't send it to me, if you think you have it, because during the *Countryman* years I did a programme for charity for Bob Long, our producer in the first series, where I did a chip-fire demonstration with the fire brigade and the quid pro quo was that we tried everything we could to get the tripe recipe. We even announced our quest with a loudspeaker at various railway stations. I got sent hundreds of tripe recipes but none of them was as good as the one I had at Salford.

After the match we all went back to the hotel and I was playing snooker when Arthur came in saying Shagger had been kidnapped. So we leapt into a taxi and said, 'The Nile Club, please,' which was where Arthur had overheard they'd gone. The taxi driver looked at me and said that he couldn't possibly take a lady to the Nile Club. Never one to be daunted by these little setbacks I said, 'Good heavens, no, I'm not a lady. I'm a madam of one of the largest brothels in London and I'm on a recruiting drive.' At which point he said, 'Right you are.' And off we went.

When we arrived at the Nile Club, I could see why he didn't want to take us there. It was the centre of the West Indian shady community in Manchester. Reggae music was playing and the only drinks they served were Newcastle Brown Ale and rum. We managed to rescue Shagger and then had to walk for miles because, unsurprisingly, there were not too many taxis hanging around the place. I read in later years that the Nile Club had burned to the ground and was not overly surprised.

Anyway, there I was in Bath, staying under the same roof as the England rugby team. I have to confess that my bedroom lay beyond the massage room so as it was quite a long corridor and as there was a chair conveniently placed outside the massage room and as I'm rather lame, I used to have to stop to rest my foot and watch the players go in and out. Sadly, most of their conversations seemed to be about how much money they could make from advertising rather than about forthcoming internationals. I did, however, manage to have a conversation with Paul Sackey and told him I thought he was wonderful, and spoke to the winger Vainikolo too. I didn't see Jonny Wilkinson, which was a great disappointment to me. The team ate in a private room rather than in the dining room, and I didn't see much of them, except that I made sure I was in the lobby in the morning when they all came down and went jogging off to the university to train. I like to think it was no coincidence that their one really good match of the season was the one immediately following this particular visit.

The recording studio was great fun. I was not the only person recording: David Tennant was there, recording something for Christmas for *Doctor Who*, and Rula Lenska, who was great company and incredibly funny, particularly about her life with Dennis Waterman and the antics they got up to, was also there. The recording took three days and was all slightly intense but the lunchtime break was always very entertaining. David Tennant was about to start rehearsals for *Hamlet* and I don't think I made myself particularly popular by saying that I always thought *Hamlet* was a play that was better read than acted. I never managed to see David Tennant in it so I don't know if his performance might have changed my opinion. Somebody once said to me of *Hamlet* that it had more clichés than any other of Shakespeare's plays and David Tennant thought this very funny when I told him but of course, they weren't clichés when Shakespeare wrote them, but have become so since.

One of the blots of being a celebrity is that your life is either feast or famine, and you can never arrange to do things when you want. This is particularly true when you're working for the BBC, who don't want you to do anything, then suddenly decide that they want something from you after all, only yesterday. Pat Llewellyn, our director on the first series of *Two Fat Ladies*, rang me up and said that BBC4 had been delighted with the success of the programme we'd made the previous year on Hannah Glasse, the eighteenth-century cook and author of *The Art of Cookery*, which was filmed at Sulgrave Manor in Oxfordshire in February. I remember it well because it was extremely cold both in the kitchen and in the outdoor shots, where my director expected me to walk through the snow, which was frosting down on me at the time, wearing nothing but an open cardigan. So I was not over-enthusiastic when Pat told me that they had another programme in mind for me, to be made at that same time of the year. It was to be on medieval cookery and, like the Hannah Glasse, it was something I was really keen to do.

The oldest known English-language cookery book is called *The Forme of Cury*. It was compiled by the master cooks, not chefs, of the courts of King Richard II and has been a book that I've always loved, cooked out of and been entertained by. For some reason so-called historical food writers have assumed that our rich ancestors, although they lived in fine buildings and owned beautiful artefacts and dressed in attractive materials, even if they did end up dry cleaning their beautiful clothes, ate dreadful food. If that's the case what did the poor eat? By and large I think the poor ate rather better then than they do nowadays. They had their allotments, their bits of land, hares were readily poachable, although they obviously couldn't take the King's deer or indeed rabbits, which were part of the living larder and were regarded as prizes for the aristocracy, and so they had access to plenty of food. But, said Optomen, the TV company, did I know a medieval kitchen where we could film?

Some years ago I had visited Gainsborough Old Hall in Gainsborough in Lincolnshire with my friend Henrietta Palmer. This had been saved by Sir Hickman Bacon and was now in the hands of English Heritage and run by the local council. I had said at the time, 'Gosh, I would love to cook in this kitchen.' And Henrietta said firmly, 'I don't think there's a prayer of that, they don't let anybody in.' So I said to Optomen, to Pat Llewellyn that I'd do it provided we could cook at Gainsborough Old Hall. With the help of Henrietta's uncle, Sir Nicholas Bacon Bt, and the local council, this was agreed. It's a perfect medieval kitchen, with an open fireplace on either side, both of them big enough to hold an ox. The Hall, which stands in the middle of Gainsborough, was built by Sir Thomas de Burgh between 1460 and 1480 and it's pretty well intact. It even has its original lavatories which used to drain into the Trent. The river has now moved due to erosion or whatever but the lavatories are still there, although happily not in use.

The Hall has a re-enactment team attached to it: Lord de Burgh's men. When I heard we were going to be using them for the filming my heart sank, because I'm not really in favour of re-enactments in historical television programmes; the ones we had in the Hannah Glasse programme, done by actors, were seedily dreadful to my mind, even though that programme was short-listed for the Glenfiddich Award. However I was wrong because Lord de Burgh's men and women were absolutely magnificent; they cooked, they did all sorts of things. Their costumes were not the rubbish that you sometimes see, made up of unlikely stuff, but were perfectly sewn using original materials. We had a beautiful young man – an aspiring actor who was still at school – who played the young King Richard II. And we also had the master cook, who sat in the middle of the kitchen on a raised seat, the only person sitting, overseeing everything.

There was one scene that sadly didn't get shown of me being taught to use a bow and arrow, which took me right back to my childhood when I learned to shoot a bow and arrow and got keen on archery. The archer I was shooting with was charming and fascinated by all the different types of arrow heads that were used for specific purposes, such as armour piercing, plate armour piercing, chainmail piercing, fire arrows, and anything else you could think of. I'm something of a believer in reincarnation, although not terribly seriously, and I asked him why he had this enthusiasm for archery. He said, 'I don't know, maybe I was there before, maybe I was at Agincourt.' And this struck me as a delightful reason for his passion.

The longbow was used to kill the King's enemies and the King's deer, and although hunting was very much a social activity, it was also a means of producing food. The only deer that would have been shot would have been roe deer, which were easier to shoot rather than hunt because they didn't run at high speed and in a straight line. A red or fallow deer would have been far too fast to get a shot off. There were other means of hunting and obtaining food which we were happy to share in the programme, called *The King's Cookbook*. Richard II's personal emblem was a greyhound and so to illustrate this John Teal, the greyhound trainer, brought down a couple of ex-coursing greyhounds, one of which, Sashy, had actually won the last Waterloo Cup, and her son, who was a magnificent big dog. I was seen walking them across a field. The scene might have ended in tears because both dogs were clearly attracted by something at the far end of the field. If you watch the programme you can see them putting their heads up and looking across the field and I have to say that if they had taken off you would have had iconic television of me being towed across the field through the mud because there was no way I could have stopped them. Greyhounds are very powerful animals, especially when they're chasing quarry. Richard II would have used greyhounds for coursing for sport, but also for hunting. A greyhound can easily bring down a deer and I have actually heard of a rather unfortunate case of a greyhound killing a swan. Swans are very powerful birds and have been known to break a grown man's leg so that gives you some estimate of the strength of the greyhound.

We were also lucky enough to have some hawks on the programme. My great friend Terry Large, who is a splendid man and chairman of the Campaign for Falconry, brought down, with some friends, a selection of hawks, including a white gyrfalcon, which is the sort of hawk that Richard II would have flown as the gyrfalcon was reserved for the King. I have watched and hawked with a variety of birds, among them the most commonplace one in daily use which is the Harris' Hawk, a Mexican hawk that hunts in packs and lives in the cactuses of the Mexican desert to stay away from the coyotes, and is not something that excites me at all. But to see a gyrfalcon, flown at the hands of Terry Large who is probably the most brilliant falconer you're ever likely to meet, was very thrilling indeed. He flew it right across the camera lens, right towards the cameraman's face, and it was beautiful to watch. They also brought a young eagle with them. I'm not keen on eagles as hawks because they're very heavy, but this one was very young and wasn't going to fly anyway. He was bonded to his owner and squawked away like a baby and huddled up to his owner in a rather endearing fashion.

When we were filming *Clarissa and the Countryman*, Terry took us on an international hawking day and on that occasion there was a Belgian house painter who had what I suppose was the Lamborghini of eagles, a Bonelli's eagle. It was a young bird, not very experienced, and when its moment came to be flown, it couldn't fly with the other hawks because there is a strict pecking order and it would merely have turned on the smaller birds. So down the hole went the ferret, out went the rabbit, up came the ferret, off went the eagle and the next thing we knew there was a horrible squealing noise and the eagle had grabbed the ferret rather than chasing the rabbit. Fortunately pet ferrets are a lot tougher than they look so if the eagle hadn't been wearing leather bands around its ankles the ferret would probably have had its foot off. The ferret then, like all Mustelidae, went into a catatonic state, spent its musk glands, which had the most terrible smell, and appeared to be dead, at which point the eagle dropped it. The owner of the ferret, rather wondering how he was going to tell his son about his pet, put it back in its box to carry it away, and five minutes later he heard banging and spitting and there was the ferret trying to get out of the box to get back at the eagle again. It was a most extraordinary scene and one that caused a certain amount of mirth after the event.

Falconry was a medieval sport that in its essence had really come back from the Crusades in the Middle East and it was a great way of bringing down wildfowl or various other birds; in the days before the shotgun, you would have hawked for pheasant and partridge. And one of the great delicacies of the Middle Ages, which we didn't for obvious reasons cook on the programme, was the heron. I've never eaten a heron, although I have eaten a moorhen, whose meat is, I think, similar and is very fishy and oily and not really terribly nice, but then one has to remember that different generations have different tastes.

Swan was a great medieval delicacy and at Gainsborough Old Hall they actually have a stuffed swan as part of the exhibition in the kitchen. I have eaten swan twice in my life, the first time when I was about ten and it was the tercentenary of William Harvey, the man who discovered the circulation of the blood. My father was president of the Harveian Society, and organised this Elizabethan banquet at Audley End, that wonderful Jacobean House in Essex. We were served all sorts of foods that they loved in medieval and Tudor times, including roasted swan. I have to say I didn't think it was very nice and I wouldn't rush to eat it again. It was rather fishy and greasy but maybe they didn't cook it properly. The second time I had it was in the west of Ireland, this time in a stew. The man who served it to us was actually driven out of the area, at that time quite a wild and superstitious part of the country, because the locals believed that the swan carried your soul to heaven so killing them was not allowed.

Once again we were filming in freezing temperatures. Celia Loewenstein, the granddaughter of the well-known food writer Ruth Loewenstein, was both an American and a vegetarian, qualities not likely to delight me, but I have to say that she was a brilliant director and the most charming person. I think we had the happiest bond between presenter and director since I filmed with Pat Llewellyn. I cooked several dishes from the King's cookbook. First was escabeche, sweet and sour fish, which was stunningly delicious, much better than the one that Gordon Ramsay gave in *The Times* that week. And it was made largely with freshwater fish, pike and tench and roach, although it also had sole. I had recently been at an event where they go round electrifying the coarse fish in a fishing river, scoop them up and take them to a pond away from the trout stream and had wondered at the time whether you could eat the roach. We used various peppers, cubit pepper and long pepper, but all the spices were ones that had been brought back from the first Crusade and from the Middle East, such as grains of Paradise, which is Ethiopian pepper because pepper as we know it was not readily available then. I have to say in this instance that the whole dish worked incredibly well.

I then went on to cook a goose stuffed with quinces and apples and chestnuts and other good things which was not easy to cook over an open fire. Indeed none of the cooking was particularly easy although I seem to have a facility for cooking over open fires, probably inherited from my mother whose great pride was that, whenever we were on a picnic, even if it was snowing or pouring with rain, she could always light a fire and cook damper bread and make billy can tea and cook other food.

So we had the goose, which was quite easily obtainable in medieval England because geese were kept for their feathers for the archers. This particular goose had been sent to us by Judy Goodman, of Goodman's Geese, who I remember happily filming with on *Two Fat Ladies*, and she does have very good geese. Finally we did pears in red wine. Now this is a dish you find on every modern restaurant menu, although it's something I don't particularly like as I always think it's rather boring; however this one, adorned with honey and all sorts of spices, was absolutely yummy. Again, it was much nicer than any of the modern versions I've had, which may have been the result of the addition of the different spices.

I was probably the only person in the performance who was warm because I spent my time, or most of it, inside the fireplace, cooking. And I realised how desirable the job in the kitchens would have been even in the summer because I don't think that the thick wall of the Old Hall would warm up very much.

The whole programme was fascinating and worked very well. I'm grateful to Sir Hickman Bacon for having saved the Old Hall. There's not a lot else to see in Gainsborough, but if you're passing up the A1 do take the detour.

In the Middle Ages people were extremely knowledgeable about using different woods, whether for cooking, utensils or tools. It's all very well for us to read how to do things, but I suppose the only way really to learn is to practise them on a daily basis. The medieval cooks knew that different woods burn at different temperatures, some quicker, some slower, some hotter. I have a wood fire at home and when I get my delivery of logs I'm always interested to see which woods burn at which temperature, and which ignite quicker. And I suppose if you were cooking on different woods every day, you'd come to know them as well as you'd know, say, an Aga, which varies so much from house to house, or the use of gas or electricity, but to a lesser degree.

They also knew which woods were best suited for which things. Elm, for instance, was often used for seats and wheels. We don't have elms now, but my childhood saw the English countryside as delineated by the elm. You'd see them at the top of a cold winter field and know they were elms. Then in the 1960s all the elms were destroyed by Dutch elm disease and the rooks had nowhere to live; what a sad time that was. Sycamore has an enzyme in it that kills bugs. Perhaps we should give up our plastic and go back to using sycamore bowls; we might have less E. coli and MRSA. Although I think that probably is down to not buying Third World meat from supermarkets. Beech and ash we use for handles that you could put strain on without it splintering. When we were cooking at Gainsborough Old Hall, we got through an awful lot of wood but it was fragmented wood, and of course the cameraman was keen for it to flare up and look dramatic so that I was trying to cook on something that I would normally have allowed to reduce back to coals.

We only think of charcoal as a fuel that we cook on in the summer months with barbecues, but again when I was young there were a lot of charcoal burners who lived deep in the woods. They were always rather grubby, slightly gypsy types. They'd take the wood and set fire to it and then cover it in mounds of earth and turfs and leave it to burn for exactly the right amount of time. And then they would sit around waiting and cooking rabbit stew and perhaps the odd poached pheasant. I used to go and visit them sometimes when I was a child and was fascinated by their lifestyle that was so tied to the days it took to make the charcoal. It wasn't a terribly profitable living but they sang and clapped and lived in their little tents in the woods and I thought it must be a wonderful life and one I would like to have joined. I expect it wasn't a wonderful life at all; we always see these things through romantic eyes. I should think they got early arthritis and didn't live very long, but it was a life that had a focus.

Incidentally, never try cooking over a coal fire, because everything comes out tasting of Lapsang Souchong. My friend Dominica has one of those wood-burning stoves and she cooks whole stews very slowly on top of it, which is a wonderful saving on cooker fuel. I gather that more and more people are installing wood stoves in their houses nowadays as the price of gas and electricity soars and supply becomes uncertain. And that's a very good thing since it not only provides work for the woodsmen and money in return for the trees on the various estates but also benefits sweeps who were beginning to be hard to find and are now growing in number.

While in Gainsborough, I stayed with my friend Henrietta Palmer, Uncle Hickey's great-great-niece, and she told me stories about him. How his mother had persuaded him not to marry, although he was a great man for the ladies, because he had tuberculosis and they all thought that he would die young. He actually lived to a fairly ripe old age and insisted on a very low-key funeral since he said that the panoply of funerals was all about snobbishness and wasn't necessary once you'd gone. He also used to put all his medicines into a box and just pull out the first one that came to hand because he said it kept his body in a constant state of curiosity as to what it was going to have next. Medics around the country will no doubt throw up their hands in horror but here was a man who was supposed to die young yet actually lived quite a long time so maybe he had a point. However, don't try this at home.

The fens of Lincolnshire have always fascinated me. I grew up on stories of Hereward the Wake fleeing into the marshes and holding off the Norman invaders for many years. They were the lands of wild men and people hiding out who found their way across the fens on hidden roads. When I was young I used to hear stories of fights where two men would have their hands tied behind their back and using their head and their teeth and their boots would fight to the death. I don't think that happens any more but certainly fifty years ago it was not uncommon.

Until the fens were drained, they supplied nothing but wildfowl and fish and particularly eels to the general market, but now Lincolnshire is a fertile county, its fields ripped from the fens and marshes by the returning Cavaliers after the restoration of Charles II. During their stay in Holland they had seen how the Dutch had reclaimed low-lying land, which they called polders, and followed suit when they came home. Wherever you go through the fens there are huge drainage ditches carrying away the water and I'm told that Lincolnshire alone could keep the country in food. Certainly in vegetables and pork products without any need for imports. Curiously, England, or Lincolnshire in particular, is the second largest producer of coriander in the world, the first being India, and we also export millions of tonnes of baby sweetcorn to China and the Far East every year. I'm frequently surprised, although I don't know why I should be, at the huge amount of Dutch influence in the fens. You find people with Dutch names – some of the bigger farming families have names like De Geest – and there's a considerable Dutch legacy in the buildings, the gables, the drainage, the ditches, and even of course the tulip fields, which are quite extensive in Lincolnshire.

Henrietta took me to meet her butcher, who I think must occupy the smallest butcher shop in Britain. His name is Mr Hardwick and he's to be found in the village of Corringham. You'll know you're in the right place because I believe there's a photograph of him and me, taken at the time of my visit, hanging proudly on his wall. I love butchers, and am honoured to be a member of the Worshipful Company of Butchers and indeed of the York Butchers' Guild, and I'm always delighted to meet one who produces really good meat. You can see some of Mr Hardwick's beef out of the back window of his shop because he sources it from a farm literally just five minutes' walk away with an excellent herd of prize cattle which go to the local abattoir nearby. And very good it was too.

One highlight while filming *The King's Cookbook* was to visit the new British Library to meet the archivist and look at the original cookbook, *The Forme of Cury*, cury being the medieval word for cooking. I suspect that as curry was really something of a British invention during the days of the Raj, it's possibly the same word applied to Indian food. Curiously, the document was a scroll, not a book, and its contents brought home, among other things, the huge amount of freshwater fish they ate in the Middle Ages. The second greatest power in the land was the Catholic Church and whether for religious reasons or simply to conserve livestock, there were something like 230 days of abstinence during the course of the year, that is days when meat must not be eaten. As a result all the great houses and the monasteries had their fish ponds. And of course there were fish in the rivers too.

We filmed a scene where I was fishing in the Trent. However if you look closely you can see that the hook is carefully hooked into a bush so that when I pull at it, it looks as though it's in the water. This was because it was the closed season for coarse fishing, when no fishing is permitted in order to allow the fish to spawn. In the middle of it, a man walked along the embankment and said, 'Eh, Clarissa, you should know better, it's the closed season.' And I pointed out to him that no fish were in danger of being caught that day. But because it scarcely fitted with the tenor of the programme, they cut it out – although I thought it was rather a charming interlude.

So the great houses had their stewponds in which they kept carp and all sorts of other freshwater fish: roach, tench, perch, zander probably (which is the pike-perch) and which formed a very important staple. We talk about fish farming now as if it were something new, but the Romans farmed fish, and I should imagine a lot of other people besides. What is wrong with modern fish farming is the pure scale of it which necessitates, for want of a better word, the pouring of chemicals into the rivers. Fascinatingly, I discovered that even farmed salmon return to the place of their birth, just as wild salmon come up the rivers to where they were born.

Bath Buns

These are to remind me of my sojourn in Bath and the English rugby team.

1lb (450g) plain flour
2 teaspoons salt
2½fl oz (60ml) milk and water in equal quantities
½oz (10g) yeast
½ tablespoon sugar
6oz (175g) butter
3 eggs
4oz (110g) chopped candied peel
2oz (50g) sultanas
1 beaten egg
2oz (50g) crushed, lumped sugar
lemon or orange peel

Preheat your oven to 220°C/425°F/ gas mark 7.

For this enriched dough, sift the flour and salt. Warm the milk and water to blood heat and cream the yeast and sugar into it. Add the butter. When the butter has melted, blend in the flour. Beat the three eggs and add, together with the candied peel and sultanas. Knead the dough and set it aside to rise until it has doubled in size. Knock it back and shape into twelve rough buns. Brush the buns with egg and sprinkle with the lumped sugar. Top with the lemon or orange peel. Leave to prove in a warm place and bake in your preheated oven for 10 to 15 minutes. An optional extra to this, if you have a good sweetshop near you, is to get some caraway comfits and top the buns with these as well as with the peel.

March

Mad March Hares in the meadow below
If they baint boxing, there'll be more snow

While still in Lincolnshire I went to visit a fascinating museum of gypsy caravans and artefacts run by a man called Gordon Boswell. I recommend it to you. And it is interesting to see how comfortable an eighteenth-century gypsy caravan was. I had remained in the county at the behest of Mark Adams to speak to a luncheon club made up of fifteen of the county's largest vegetable growers and farmers. Let me tell you a bit about the Adamses. I came to be friends in a rather roundabout way. George Adams, Mark's father, who I met at Gray's Inn, was the most wonderful man, the picture of the perfect Lincolnshire farmer: he wore a pork pie hat, drove an old Bentley and kept a wonderful table. Together with his wife Joan, their parties were brilliant and heavily centred as you might imagine towards meat in general and pork in particular. George had inherited thirty butcher shops in the county and, seeing the way the world was going, had sold all but one of them which he kept purely and simply to provide him with perfect hams and pork pies, excellent haslet and delicious Lincolnshire chine. Chine, I should tell you, is a strange dish peculiar to the Lincolnshire fens which is a pig's neck cut down the middle and collared and stuffed with parsley. It's traditionally eaten at harvest time, and Johnny Scott used to get one for teas for the men who came in to help him with the lambing.

I'm reminded of a curious instance, which shows you just how little you can trust MAFF (as Defra, the Department of Environment, Food and Rural Affairs, then was), when they translated an EU regulation which, in the translation they offered, would have made it illegal to make and sell chine. The man in Boston who ran the largest producer of chine in the county, and whose business would have been in ruins if the regulation went through, hired himself an international lawyer and a translator and, lo and behold, when the EU regulation was properly translated, it did not preclude the making of chine at all. Which just goes to show, don't trust whatever passes for our Ministry of Agriculture.

To return to the Adamses, Johnny Scott and I were at Goodwood House for a publisher's evening which Headline was hosting when it was about to publish the first *Clarissa and the Countryman* book in 2000. After dinner a small, lively person came up to me and asked if we were going to Spalding. Our publicist at the time said, 'No, of course not and where's Spalding anyway?' I was rather annoyed by this and so I said to Christine, the lively person, 'If you ask us, we will come.' The publicist said, 'No, you won't.' I told her, 'Look, there's nothing to stop us going to Lincolnshire on our own. It doesn't have to be part of our organised book tour.'

So Johnny and I went to Lincolnshire that year and there in this delightful shop in the middle of Spalding was a huge crowd of people; they were practically hanging from the rafters, and we did our talk and afterwards we sold the largest number of books – ninety-eight, I think – I have ever managed at such an event. We signed more books for stock as well and each time I have been back there I've had a marvellous reception. The bookshop was under the auspices of George Adams who I think owned the property and so we were invited to his house for dinner afterwards with a large assortment of other people including various relatives. George was feeling a bit under the weather, so he asked Johnny if he would carve the ham which was a most tremendous compliment. Fortunately Johnny is one of the world's best carvers.

I met George's son Mark through shooting at the Pointons' in Staffordshire. He's an excellent shot who shoots with a pair of Purdey 20-bores among other guns and was forever mobbing me up about my little 16-bore hammer gun and asking why I didn't go and get a proper gun. My gun has an under-lever action, which makes reloading it rather a slow process, and it also has hammers which you have to pull back and cock before firing.

Then the most curious thing happened. After George had sold his shops, he went into pig production and became one of the largest pig producers in Europe. It wasn't the sort of pork that I would choose to buy, although there was nothing wrong with it, and it was British bred, but simply because it was too lean and from breeds that were specially reared for the commercial market. George might have continued like this had it not been that he became very ill and, in the end, he died. Mark took over the business but also became ill and during his convalescence he decided that he didn't want to spend the rest of his life on the mass production of pigs and all the problems that went with it so he sold the business to Tulip. The merger was so large that it had to go through the Monopolies and Mergers Commission. George continued with his one shop and focused on breeding unusual strains of pig and on producing perfect pork pies and other Lincolnshire delicacies. Today these pork pies sell into Fortnum and Mason among other outlets, and are quite excellent. As a result we became friends because he had moved into a world I was familiar with.

It was interesting to meet the vegetable growers and the farmers at the luncheon club and we discussed many aspects of vegetable production including, of course, organic. When I was running the catering at Lennoxlove, the seat of the Duke of Hamilton, we grew our own vegetables for the café in the gardens there which had always been organic. The old Duchess of Hamilton, the present Duke's mother, had been a friend of Eve Balfour, the original organicist who had her spiritual awakening over a compost heap in East Lothian. Before her time, of course, there had been no need for organic produce because there weren't any chemicals to speak of. I think that properly grown and freshly harvested organic vegetables probably do take the prize and are delicious, but for the purposes of commercial growing what is important in my opinion is best practice. If you go into the supermarkets in this country you will find that an awful lot of the organic produce comes from countries not governed by the Soil Association which means that in some cases they can be registered just three days before they are harvested and up to that moment can have been systematically sprayed. They simply aren't worth the extra money. And of course the EU regulations about the size, conformity and perfection of vegetables that are allowed to be sold means that there is always a question mark hanging over any organic vegetable or fruit produce. If you grow your own vegetables you'll know perfectly well that vegetables don't grow in straight lines or achieve perfect shapes and don't taste any the worse for that. Moreover, if you buy in supermarkets, the fruit and vegetables have all been chilled and irradiated and generally preserved so that they don't sprout or go soft on you, and this is equally true of organic produce, because once they are harvested what happens to them is a whole different ball game.

We also talked about importation. As I said earlier, Lincolnshire could probably keep the whole country fed in vegetables but the supermarkets, who, incidentally, have bought up quite large areas of land in central Europe, prefer to buy their vegetables from abroad because labour laws in other parts of the world mean that produce can be grown more cheaply there. There is also the question of pesticides. If you go to the south of Spain, you will see miles and miles and miles of plastic greenhouses, all growing vegetables that are tended and harvested by North Africans who the Spanish allow in simply to work on these crops. The workers are not allowed into the towns, they're not allowed anywhere else, and they live in shack communities around the vegetable houses. And of course the vegetables are all systematically sprayed which can't do the Africans much good either and certainly by the time we get the vegetables I'd really rather not eat them.

Spain is a European country within the EU so how much worse might the practices be in countries over which we have no control? In my opinion one of the advantages of producing and growing vegetables, meat or whatever in our own country is that even if you object to some of the practices of our farmers, you can at least do something about it. Years ago I used to go to South America to oversee cattle sales from Australia and in South America they don't kill animals infected with foot and mouth, and nor, I think, do they in Africa. So that if the beast survives, it continues to run with the herd and you see animals in a very parlous state indeed. But if those animals are fattened up, they will be killed and sent to us.

The last great foot and mouth epidemic in 2001 was supposed to have been caused by African beef. Tony Blair had decided that the army were no longer to eat British beef but African beef instead, which they could import more cheaply. This got into the scrap buckets of the army on the Northumberland ranges and so into the swill processing of the farm at Heddon-on-the-Wall, to whom they traced the outbreak. This is probably because the farmer was not boiling up his swill to a high enough temperature, since he had been prosecuted on several previous occasions and moved farms. But there's no doubt that that was the source of the outbreak. The latest outbreak in 2007, of course, was the result of sloppy practices at government plants where they were manufacturing the virus. None of this would have happened if we were not importing beef. It's all very well to say that foot and mouth does not translate to humans, but this is not strictly true. It rarely translates to humans. I remember many years ago being at a court in Hampshire where the defendant's mitigation for driving erratically on his scooter was that he was indeed suffering from foot and mouth and there was medical evidence to prove it.

Tony Blair's government, having announced at the time of their installation twelve years ago that they would do to the farmers what the Conservatives did to the miners, are not going to remedy any of the flaws in the policy of importation. If our farmers have survived the last twelve years, it is no thanks to Mr Blair's government. I continue to regard it as Mr Blair's government since of course Mr Brown was never elected as Prime Minister; all he has ever been elected as is an MP who was then appointed Chancellor of the Exchequer, and we'll come to his record on that later, shall we.

I had an interesting and entertaining day with my fifteen farmers and received a delightful present from Mark Adams for my pains. He collects meat skewers and has an interesting array of all different shapes and sizes and ages, but the one he gave me, which was presumably for cooking hare, was a small game skewer with a greyhound running along the top.

Coming back to greyhounds, March of this year will always remain for me Sonic's extra month. Those of you who have read my *Clarissa's Comfort Food* will perhaps have noticed that it is dedicated to a greyhound called Sonic. Her running name was Holy Ground Girl and in 1999 she won the Anglia Cup and three weeks later went to the Waterloo Cup where she was sadly knocked out in one of the earlier rounds, but she was, I think, the dog I loved most in all my life. She didn't belong to me unfortunately, but to my friend, Sally Merison. She was the most enchanting dog: witty, soft, consoling and at this point very consoling, because I was still struggling to write *Comfort Food* and, not having a kitchen as you know, I went to Sally's to practise recipes. I don't say invent, because most of the recipes in that book I had already invented years before. Sonic's only vice to my mind was that she was a thief; most greyhounds are thieves, most lurchers are thieves too, probably through their greyhound blood, but she was one par excellence. She could whip a pheasant with all its feathers on off a table and when you turned again she had plucked the bird and was happily eating it.

At my sixtieth birthday party she sneaked through the crowds waiting to hurl themselves at the buffet and was seen bearing off a very splendid steak. This was particularly amazing because she had no teeth. They had been removed earlier for her own good to prevent further infection and it was amazing what she could do without teeth. Devour a hamburger in its bun, for instance. Anyway, Sonic's place was on a bed under the kitchen window. If she wasn't outside, happily wagging her tail and barking greetings at passers-by in this fairly remote part of the country, she was sleeping peacefully on her bed. By now she'd become an old dog and Sally had made the decision that the time had come to send her to the heavenly coursing fields in the sky.

So we were sitting around rather glumly because the vet was coming the next day, but Sonic, being unaware of this, was quite happy. She had lost condition because she had cut her foot which had got infected and hadn't responded to antibiotics and although it had healed up, she'd become very lame. Sally took her up the river for one last walk before the vet was due and because she was so lame didn't put her on a lead. At this point, a roe deer got in front of her, and off went Sonic up the towpath in hot pursuit, moving as lithely and enthusiastically as she had in her running days. Sally came back and told me this and I said, 'For heaven's sake, ring the vet.' So she rang the vet who said, 'Well, we won't do it today then, will we.' And Sally collected some painkillers, and Sonic had an extra month where she was incredibly well and energised and flirty and silly, back to her old self and playing with her little friend, Kipper.

Sonic was not only a prize-winning greyhound, she was also the mother of, in total, twelve pups but in one litter she produced ten. They all lived and she actually grew a pair of extra nipples in order to feed them. I think by the time they went to their various homes she was quite glad to see the back of them, but she was the most brilliant mother and the pups had a wonderful time, running riot all over Sally's paddock and garden. Anyway, Sonic had a lovely extra month. She was much spoiled by Sally and myself and given all sorts of nice things to eat and on 24 April she went to her rest; it was a great privilege to have known her, and she runs through my dreams.

If you have the room, and you really don't need too much room, greyhounds make the most perfect house pets. Contrary to expectations, they don't need a huge amount of exercise: one good walk a day is quite enough. And having been bred for the great Halls, they're happy to sit or lie around all day greeting visitors. They have excellent people skills and they look sufficiently alarming to scare people off with a surprisingly deep bark. Coursing greyhounds tend to be re-homed either with their owners or with their owners' friends but the racing world produces quite a large surplus of greyhounds so if you're looking for a dog, get on to one of the greyhound re-homing centres and treat yourself to the company of one of these charming dogs.

Now let me tell you about Kipper, my second favourite dog in the world, and my first who is a Border terrier who fishes. Other Border terriers chase rats and rabbits or whatever, but not Kipper: his great love is fish. Whether he was a fisherman in a previous existence, who knows, but the first time I went fishing at Sally's, she said, 'Kipper will go with you,' and I slightly bit my lip because you don't really want to take a terrier if you're going up a clear chalkstream where the fish sees you coming. Anyway, I went through the gate and shut it firmly behind me. Kipper went underneath it, and bounced along. I stopped to look at the river and Kipper sat down beside me. Suddenly I felt a bang on my leg and I looked down and there was Kipper pointing. I looked to where he was pointing and there indeed was a fish on the fin.

Kipper has a further talent as a retriever. If you catch a fish, in he will go, and land it for you. He can land anything up to three pounds, without any damage to the fish. He has a mouth like a Labrador. It's the most remarkable thing; I've never come across it anywhere else. There is a mill-stream by the house, and when nobody's prepared to take Kipper fishing, he will lean nonchalantly on the wall of the mill-stream, watching the big fish swimming about. There are certain people who take him fishing and he knows instinctively when it is the alternate Monday that he goes fishing, not every Monday, and even who is coming. He does not, however, like gráyling so when the grayling season comes, people are reluctant to take him, for obvious reasons, as you will have to land your own fish, and if you do, he'll probably pee on it. It's the terrier code, isn't it? If it moves, kill it; if it's edible, eat it; if it's female, well you know what; and if it doesn't move, pee on it. But what is really bizarre is that if it's trout, the only other fish to be caught on the fly on the Dever, Kipper won't pee on it.

Venison Scotch Eggs

These venison Scotch eggs were something I developed with James Gibbs, brother of Wiggy, and remind me of the Scotch eggs that I took, along with the pork pies, to supplement our inedible dinner at the Nibbie Awards.

This makes eight Scotch eggs.

8 hard-boiled eggs
flour
1 dessertspoon fennel seeds, crushed
12oz (350g) venison minced as for sausage
meat with 4oz (110g) fat pork
2 eggs
breadcrumbs
fat or oil for frying

Dust the hard-boiled eggs lightly with the flour. Mix the crushed fennel seeds into the sausage meat and divide the meat into eight equal rounds. Wrap the sausage meat lightly round each egg, sealing the edges firmly. Beat the raw eggs lightly and roll the wrapped eggs in them before coating with breadcrumbs. Heat the fat or oil until smoking and deep-fry the eggs until golden brown. Alternatively, shallow-fry to seal and place on a rack on a tray in the oven, and cook at 220°C/425°F/gas mark 7 for 10 to 15 minutes until they are done.

April

Don't cast a clout till May is out

It was cream that brought me to Hungerford and what was to prove one of the happiest days of the year, on 1 April, but let us start with the cream. I had first encountered Prosperous Farm when attending Winchester's fantastic farmers' market with my friend Carrots. Her daughter, Lucy, was mad about their wonderful Guernsey milk. I thought the name rang a bell and cried, 'Jethro Tull!' which raised a smile from the man behind the stall. I do not mean the rural comedian of course, but the much earlier inventor of the seed drill, a former barrister of Gray's Inn, my Inn of Court, and one of the heroes of the Agricultural Revolution. In 1701, Jethro bought Prosperous Farm and established a Guernsey dairy herd. Less well known than his treatise on horse husbandry, or an eighteenth-century cure for insomnia, his work on Guernsey cows remains to this day one of the mainstays of the industry. What of course Jethro didn't know is that the milk of Guernsey cows, along with that of the African Zebu cattle, contains an enzyme that cures, or at least strongly alleviates, asthma.

I could rant on for hours on the subject of milk, but will try to keep it short. I can remember learning at a very early age the line, 'Milk is called the perfect food, which it isn't, but it almost is.' I'm of the generation that got free milk for elevenses before Thatcher, milk-snatcher, did away with it. I have always loved milk and when I was a child had spectacular nightmares from the cheese I used to sneak from the larder. When I was about nine we went skiing in Megève and I was passionate about the Reblochon cheese. I vaguely remember Mont Blanc as a backdrop to the resort but I clearly remember the cheese. The nutritionists, who seem not to read the more technical books I plough through on your behalf – Harold McGee, McCance and Widdowson, and most recently, Barry Groves's *Trick and Treat* – have all jumped or been bribed by free trips abroad or holidays on to the olive oil path and the 1980s saw the condemnation of dairy products, an attitude that is only now just beginning to swing back.

Louis Pasteur was commissioned to study spoilage in the French wine industry and developed pasteurisation, a method of heating to destroy microbes which was also applied to milk and therefore did us something of a disservice. The heating destroys not only the harmful microbes that might lead to TB, or brucellosis undular fever (spontaneous abortion), but also the benevolent microbes that help prevent allergies and provide more calcium to the bones. In fact, the more you mess around with milk, the less good it does you. I remember in the late eighties there was an outbreak of rickets in the affluent borough of Hampstead. The luvvies had been feeding their children skimmed milk. 'No!' they cried. 'It cannot be rickets; that is a disease of the Victorian poor.' The Royal Free Hospital pointed out that it was in fact a disease caused by calcium deficiency. The nutritionist will tell you that there is more calcium in skimmed than semi-skimmed milk but it is of course the fat in the milk that helps the absorption of calcium into the bones. I know of only one place where you can buy unpasteurised, whole milk, which is Middle Farm, Firle, on the A27 Lewes to Eastbourne road. Go and buy some, and taste it; it is delicious and quite different, and if you use it for sauces or rice pudding or other milk puddings it is sensational, better than anything you've ever eaten and fit for a queen.

I first made my way to Prosperous Home Farm up the Salisbury–Hungerford road on a late spring morning. The new grass was lush in the paddocks and so vividly green that it almost hurt the eyes and the Guernsey cows, with that pretty dried apricot and white colouring, wandering around enjoying it made a fetching picture. I drove into the yard and was greeted by a man who I now know is called Derek and has become a good acquaintance on my trips to Hungerford. There is a fridge cupboard from which you can help yourself if there's no one around, and leave your money in the honesty box. Prosperous does full milk, semi-skimmed milk – though I have to say the semi-skimmed is probably richer than most full cream milk you get in shops – home-made yoghurt and, best of all, double cream. Prosperous cream, I would argue, is the best in the world. When I had my sixtieth birthday party last year, pudding was locally grown strawberries and raspberries with Prosperous cream and everybody who tasted it and didn't already know it, raved about its virtues and how delicious it was. It is rich, golden, unctuous and just simply the best.

They also make a blue cheese which I'm told is regarded as impossible using Guernsey milk, because the milk is simply too rich to make cheese, but I had a couple of these cheeses at my birthday party and they were really quite good. In the yard where I went into the farm shop, there were some pretty little Berkshire piglets with their dainty white tiptoes in a pen, but also one or two of the calves that had been weaned from their mothers. The whole place was quite delightful. In the

best traditions of Jethro Tull, Prosperous is now the passion of
Rod Kent, a city businessman and banker who regards it as his
pride and joy and is forever trying to produce newer and better
products from his herd.

With my car stuffed with goodies, I left Prosperous behind
and made my way to Hungerford. At the time I knew nothing
about it, and if I associated it with anything, it was that dreadful
incident back in 1987 when they had a gunman run riot. Today
Hungerford is one of the few places in the British Isles where
I could seriously consider living. It is a quite remarkable town
unscathed by supermarkets and part of its individuality lies in
the fact that since John of Gaunt in the fourteenth century it has
belonged to itself, and has had no manor or lordship or abbey
in ascendancy over it. John of Gaunt, in exchange for housing
an army, which he was taking through to drive the French off
the Isle of Wight, gave the common lands and the rivers of the
meadows to the citizens of Hungerford and so it has remained
until the present day. I learned all this from a delightful couple
called Tyrell and Cathy Bossom, who own the needlework
shop in Hungerford. It's difficult these days to find a really good
shop for tapestries and this, I'm happy to say, is one of the best.
So if I had no other reason for going to Hungerford, this would
provide it.

But there are plenty of other reasons. It has a very good
bookshop, an independent one, and a very good wine merchant
with an unusual choice of wine. I found two of my brother's
favourite wines, Château Enfant Jésus, referred to in my family
as Château Baby Je, with a picture of the infant of Prague on its
label, and Château Mouche, which means fly and has flies on
the label, as though they had just landed on the bottle. The town
also has a fine silversmith who stocks both antique and modern

silver and where I've been lucky enough to buy some lovely presents for people. There's a delicatessen that promises much, but sadly it's almost impossible to get served in, a butcher and a greengrocer, all within easy walking distance of each other; two cafés, the one down near the silversmith owned by the former Mayor, Barbara Bar, the first woman Mayor of Hungerford. What sadly the town doesn't have is a decent pub or restaurant that's going to encourage you to stop there and eat, or at least not one that I have found on my multiple visits.

It was through the Bossoms that I was introduced to Barbara Bar and she asked me if I would speak at a Hochtide lunch on 1 April. Hochtide is an ancient tradition where the rules governing the town's tenants and the rights of the commoners to grazing and fishing are read out loud at the court-leet because it was assumed in the fourteenth century that the commoners would not necessarily be able to read, and so they are still read out to this day.

The day of the lunch was bright and sunny. I had not gone the night before to witness the ale tasting, a ritual left over from the Middle Ages which was no doubt to license those people within the town who were allowed to make and sell ale and to check the quality of their product. Nowadays, it's just a jolly. But on the actual Hochtide day, after the court meeting and the reading out of the names of the tenants to see who is in attendance and who has paid their penny for not attending, the Tutti-men are sent out.

Tutti is a word that causes much argument among experts, but the general consensus is that it is an abbreviation of tithing, and the men are sent out round all the tenants to collect the rent wearing garlanded hats and carrying poles adorned with floral posies and oranges stuck with cloves. The oranges, I understand, symbolise William of Orange, who planned the glorious and bloodless revolution of 1689 in the town of Hungerford because, having no lord of the manor, there was no one person who could have been charged with treason if things had gone wrong. I suspect that the posies on the poles were to guard them against the stench of some of the poorer parts of town in days gone by.

The highlight of today is the feast at the lunch at which I was bidden to speak. Usually such occasions provide really rather horrible food. I am tired to death of the rubber chicken and disgusting, ready-made sauces that you get at other events and I often think I will say, yes I'll speak, but please can I bring my own lunch, or please can I not come to dinner? In this instance, it was entirely different. We had smoked trout, from trout caught in the Kennet, the local river, followed by very good beef which had been grazed on the common and the pudding was made with locally garnered fruits and, of course, Prosperous cream. It was all quite delicious.

After the speeches, the farrier came in to shoe the new arrivals, those people who'd not been to the lunch before. You go and you put your foot up and the blacksmith proceeds to hammer a horseshoe into the sole of your shoe until you shout, 'Punch!' At which point you pay a nominal sum of money and are given the shoe and the nail, which of course has not been driven into your foot, and you take it away as a souvenir. Some people had their nails adorned with enamel red roses, so I think they were probably part of the court, the red rose being a symbol of John of Gaunt. The Tutti-men come back during lunch to report on their morning's garnerings and are presumably given something to eat. At the end of the proceedings, the ale that was tasted the night before has been made into a punch and is served round to all and sundry, except me, of course, although I did smell it, and it smelled very good indeed.

But the ever dreadful loom of Health and Safety had spread its tentacles over the day. In previous years, warmed pennies had been thrown out to the children of the town for them to scrabble for and take home. However Health and Safety decided that this was unsafe and so the event had to be cancelled. One rather hopes that in this credit crunch and world crisis that are afflicting us at the moment that one of the first losses among government jobs would be in Health and Safety but somehow I doubt it. They do represent to me the worst excesses of Big Brother society, let alone the nanny state. By Big Brother, I don't mean the television programme, but George Orwell's *1984*. I remember one occasion at Lennoxlove, when Callum Bannerman, the chief executive officer, was showing the Health and Safety officer into the kitchens and I came through to meet him. I was not cooking, I was merely there to discuss with him our planned alterations to the kitchen, and what we were allowed to do. As I stuck out my hand to shake his he looked at it disdainfully and said, 'You didn't wash your hands.' If I washed my hands every time I shook hands with a Health and Safety officer, I'd turn into Lady Macbeth. In any event the impact on the town of Hungerford was that the children were denied their pennies. I can't understand why Health and Safety didn't simply say that you can throw the coins but you can't heat them, but maybe they thought that scrabbling for them was also dangerous.

One of the more curious conflicts facing Hungerford at the moment concerns their common rights. Tony Blair's rather unpleasant and, to my mind, fascist government sneaked through hundreds and hundreds of Acts during his term in office. One

of these was designed to limit the rights of common lands and
bring them under statute so that they could be administered by
Defra. This of course overturns traditions that go back to the
time at which the mind of man runneth not, as the old legal
maxim used to say. In the case of Hungerford, Hungerfordees
receive their rights by royal charter, which is therefore not
revocable by statute. Defra are now trying to get Hungerford to
sign away their rights in exchange for some sort of grant. This
is the organisation that drained so much water out of the River
Kennet for the town of Swindon, or allowed it to be done, that
at one point there was almost no water in the upper reaches of
the Kennet. I think Hungerford will be well advised to stay out
of the hands of Defra. One of the speeches at the lunch was very
much along the lines of, 'Be very very careful; he who dines
with the devil needs a long spoon. He who dines with Defra
shouldn't go anywhere near the table at all.'

I was struck during the reading of the regulations of the
court by how careful they were to cover every eventuality; for
instance, if you were allowed to keep horses on the common
grazing you must not have a rig (an improperly cut gelding
that displays stallion-type behaviour), nor must you have a
mare who had aborted. The mare was not allowed to be put on
the land for twenty-eight days after the abortion. These are all
medieval regulations that have a great deal more understanding
of the actuality of things than any modern-day government
organisation. There are also regulations as to what fish you
can take and at what time of the year, obviously to allow for
the breeding season. I loved these traditions, which in many
places have become nothing more than a nostalgic frivol, but in
Hungerford they remain very much at the centre of the town.
It is the pride that the citizens of Hungerford take in themselves

and their traditions that particularly delighted me and I had the most wonderful day.

At the end they gave me a day's fishing on the Kennet as a present for speaking. I was most grateful for this. I'd really rather people didn't give me things when I speak because very often I'm travelling and it's difficult to find room in my car. Sometimes people give me flowers. Now please don't take offence if in the last few years you've given me flowers, but actually I rather dislike cut flowers. This is no slight on the flowers but I have suffered from chronic hay fever since the age of eighteen and also, what do you do with a large bunch of cut flowers, even ones that are in plastic water buckets, if you are driving round and round the country? I don't always have a host I can give them to either. On one rather embarrassing occasion I actually succeeded in starting a roadside shrine, because the flowers were so sporous that I got out of my car and left them by the side of the road, hoping that somebody would pick them up and take them home to make good use of them. When I drove past along the same road ten days later, there was my bunch of flowers, surrounded by many other bunches of flowers. Obviously somebody thought there had been a death there and so the whole thing had built up.

The other present that people give me is hampers of food, which is very nice especially if they contain local produce which I'm always delighted to have. The only trouble is that very often they include items that I'd be pleased to have if I was at home, such as venison kidneys which people have read that I like, or local smoked fish. But sometimes I'm not going to be home for three or four weeks so then I have to find a good home for these foods. It makes me sound awfully ungrateful and really I'm not, I do appreciate the good intentions behind all these gifts but I would be perfectly happy if you gave me nothing at all. However if you insist on giving me a present, a box of Sally Clark's truffles, which you can order by post, will keep me very happy and thinking well of you for years to come.

I'm still looking forward to my fishing on the Kennet which I couldn't take last season because of my eyes. I became aware in the spring of the year that my eyesight was deteriorating, because I was finding it harder to read signposts on my excursions. I simply assumed that the time had come when I would need glasses so, as the advert says, I went to Specsavers. They couldn't have been nicer and more helpful and told me that I didn't need glasses. There was only one thing wrong with my eyes and that was the fact that I had cataracts, but they were not yet ripe enough for operation. Curiously, I'm exactly the same age as my grandmother was when she had her cataracts done. I'm very like my grandmother physically and I have to say that for the rest of her life she never wore glasses, and she died at the age of eighty-seven. She only had to use a magnifying glass to read the small print in the racing stud books. So this bodes well for the future.

Hungerford served a delicious lunch – sadly, something of an exception – and I'm constantly mystified at how much bad food is served in this country since presumably it takes as much effort to create good food as it does to serve something really rather unpleasant. I was reminded of this twice in the year because *Spilling the Beans* was nominated for a couple of awards. The first was biography of the year at the Nibbies, the British Book Awards, although I didn't win on that occasion, the prize going to Russell Brand. We went to Grosvenor House for this huge, over-heated do, over-heated because the air-conditioning never works in the banqueting room of the Grosvenor House.

But I was forewarned that the food would be disgusting because it is the biggest function room in London, outside, I suppose, the Livery Halls and they really don't give a stuff. I remember when I was chairman of the Game Conservancy Trust we held a Game Conservancy Ball there, for which Marco Pierre White had offered to do the food but was refused because the hotel insisted on doing it.

On this occasion I therefore went to Fortnum and Mason and bought half a dozen of their very good, large pork pies which were supplied by Mark Adams, who I mentioned earlier, and half a dozen Scotch eggs, which were also excellent, and I arrived at Grosvenor House with my Fortnum's bag containing all these goodies. It was quite funny, because as you go into the entrance to Grosvenor House for an event like this, there are dozens and dozens of cameras, press cameras and the general public, all taking photographs of glamorous people arriving and there was me clutching my Fortnum and Mason's bag. My trouble is I really should have been a high court judge because I don't own a television set, or I didn't until the Olympics anyway, and I never know who any of these so-called celebrities are. I'm always surprised how many people know who I am. So I found myself having my photograph taken with an excessively good-looking gentleman, who turned out to be somebody from *Dragons' Den*. Another one of those programmes that I've never really understood the point of. These occasions are long-drawn-out, self-congratulatory affairs and I was very glad of my pork pies and Scotch eggs, as indeed was everybody else at my table, because what we were served to eat was a rather nasty plate of hors d'oeuvres, for want of a better description, which I can only assume came from Brake Bros.

Having sworn that I would never attend another such event, later in the year I was very honoured to be nominated and indeed won the Independent Booksellers' Book of the Year Award. I am an independent bookseller myself and have been for a great many years, and although I don't presently have a shop I still consider myself to be one. As of course I had to be present, I had to sit and eat my way through a disgusting rubber chicken dinner, having been unable to buy any comestibles beforehand. However I was very pleased to win the prize, which was voted for by the booksellers themselves rather than by a committee and they declared that mine was the book that had been most helpful to their businesses during the past year. Sadly, what I got was a green glass plaque, quite nicely engraved, rather than one of the Nibbies, which are sort of giant gilt pen nibs that I had rather fancied passing on to my agent Heather Holden-Brown to keep in her office because they're quite quirky.

The award dinner was held in the Metropole Hotel in Brighton where I had what must have been one of their best suites which overlooked the sea and was really rather beautiful. I haven't been to the Metropole for years, but I was at school in Brighton, or in Hove, I should say, and the Metropole was one of the places we used to go, sometimes for lunch or certainly for tea.

The countryside was yellow as I drove through it on the way to Brighton, yellow with field upon field of rape. I hate rape – well, I hate rape in any usage of the word – but as a lifelong hay fever sufferer, I particularly hate the rather nasty spores plant. I remember the year I went into treatment, I went in on 9 April and the rape was just beginning to show its head and by the time I left on 23 June it was in full flower and waiting to be harvested. When I see the rape glaring in the fields these days, it always reminds me of a young man I was in treatment with called Scott, who was only seventeen when he came into the recovery centre, Promis. He had been Junior Tenpin Bowling Champion of Britain and he was a beautiful young man who took to glue sniffing – solvent abuse. I want to tell you this because I was amazed recently to discover a Member of Parliament, a man who'd been a cabinet minister, who had never heard of solvent abuse, and I thought maybe I should say something about it.

The habit is confined largely to the young, to teenagers, and people usually move on to stronger substances after a while. Curiously, Scott couldn't bear the smell of fish because fish-bones are part and parcel of an awful lot of glues and it reminded him of his addiction. He was doing well at Promis and everybody thought that he was stabilised and so people were given back their canisters of shaving foam and hairspray which of course are another source of solvents for the addict. He relapsed on the gas from somebody's spray deodorant and had to leave. He was allowed back which was unusual and this was largely because of his youth. Scott came from the sort of family where you would expect that problems might arise. His stepmother once sent his mother a package by post, all wrapped up as a birthday present, and when she opened it, inside was a poisonous tarantula. Fortunately she wasn't injured, but you can imagine the impact, not only on her, but on Scott. He went through Promis and got better and went out into the world, but I'm sorry to say that on his eighteenth birthday he killed himself in the park where he used to play as a child. I should also tell you that Promis is no more; the treatment centre that helped me and so many others, under Doctor Robert Lefever, was a victim of the credit crunch. Partly, I understand, because Kent

County Council lost so much money investing in Iceland that it couldn't pay its bills and that was one bridge too far.

Nowadays, rape comes into flower in March. I imagine it's a different variety so I have to trot off and get my hay fever prescription that much earlier. I know people who have never suffered from hay fever and then when a rape field was planted next door to them have suddenly acquired it, in one instance a lady who was well into her seventies at the time.

The reason for the increase in fields of rape is that Defra instructed farmers to plant it because the government was very keen on bio-diesel. We've also seen pictures of the cabinet or Prime Minister, be it Blair or Brown, driving around in rather large 4 x 4 bio-diesel-powered Land-Rovers. Not for them the neat little cars that zip around using almost no fuel at all. That would not fit in with the pomposity of the occasion. The only trouble is that the government has failed to encourage or give incentives for producing bio-fuel in this country so that at the time of writing there is nobody who is producing bio-fuel in the United Kingdom. One or two plants have been opened and then closed again because they were simply not economically viable. As a result, all this rape, once it has been cut, is loaded into diesel tankers and shipped to Germany where it is turned into bio-fuel. It is then re-loaded into diesel tankers and shipped back again, thereby undoing any possible benefit to greenhouse warming, carbon footprints or the like, along the way. In fact the amount of fuel and energy that has been consumed in producing this bio-diesel is quite terrifying to contemplate.

There was a huge kerfuffle a year or so ago because there was not enough grain, as a result of the increase in rape production, if you remember, to fatten animals for the supermarkets. People from whom I buy my meat turn the animals out on to grass in the summer and supplement their food as little as possible, which of course takes longer. Therefore the supermarkets, who want their meat quickly on those occasions when they are not importing it, buy it from people who are fattening it rapidly. Defra had failed to do their sums and therefore there was not enough feed available for fattening.

When I was sitting on a platform at the Bath and West Show, the very enchanting and delightful Meurig Raymond, who is deputy of the National Farmers' Union, was advocating the growing of rape for bio-diesel. I pointed out that that was the reason why there was a shortage of grain, because all this stuff was being shipped to Germany to be turned into bio-fuel. He replied with great enthusiasm that at the end of processing rape there is, of course, a cattle cud left that you can feed to cattle. With great glee I said that the cattle cud would be in Germany and I doubted they were going to ship it back to us for free. And in any event yet more fuel would be used in shipping it back to us.

I am very ambivalent about the whole question of global warming and greenhouse gases or anything similar. To my mind it seems that in this country at least they are rods with which to beat us and provide us with fewer services while demanding more taxes. The life I lead is by accident quite ecological. I don't have central heating; if I'm cold I put on a woollen jumper. One of the things that annoys me most is these artificial fleeces that people wear. Fleece, as far as I understand it, is the wool of a sheep or another such animal. Whereas these artificial ones are made on the other side of the world, mostly in China, from synthetic material, using quite a lot of chemicals and energy, and then shipped back to the United Kingdom to be sold very cheaply thanks to the slave labour involved in their manufacture.

They're not particularly warm, unlike wool which gets warmer as it gets wetter, and are not in any way weatherproof.

I remember when we were making *Clarissa and the Countryman*, we were filming this sort of picnic by a large bonfire on the Isle of Mull, eating the various foods that we had gathered while on the island, langoustines, venison and so forth. The BBC crew and the production team, who had all spent their allocated money for outdoor wear on clothes like snowboarding jackets and fleeces, stood around shivering in the rain, while Johnny and I, who were dressed in tweeds and loden cloth, got happily warmer as we got wetter. It obviously doesn't last for ever, but it is a very good example of its qualities. And it does of course give the sheep farmers an income.

From the Middle Ages onwards, the fortunes of Britain were grown on the back of the sheep. It is the reason why the Lord Chancellor sits on a woolsack. As far as I understand it, the Lord Chancellor still sits on a woolsack; it hasn't been emptied out and filled with synthetic fibres. And he's still the Lord Chancellor because this particularly stupid Labour government under Mr Blair did away with the Lord Chancellor only to discover that they couldn't actually do so because the complications would be far too great for the constitution or lack of it, and so they very quietly reinstated him. I was interested to see Jack Straw, one-time card-carrying Communist, at the State Opening of Parliament dressed in full regalia. I couldn't see if he was wearing silk stockings and knee breeches but he was certainly in full robes kneeling to the Queen to hand her the speech and backing away down the steps in the most traditional of manners. There was a time in my life when I was a blue-badged tourist guide and, believe me, the tourists don't come to this country to look at the politicians in their suits. They come for the pomp and circumstance if they come at all.

A few years ago when we were again filming *Clarissa and the Countryman*, it was interesting to discover that the main market for the fleeces of black-faced sheep was the Italian bridal bed market. Apparently in Italy it was good luck and a promise of fertility to have an under-blanket made from the fleece of black-faced sheep and brides would go out to warehouses with their bridesmaids, and presumably their mothers, to choose a suitable fleece.

The Russian rouble had declined in 2000, but fortunately for the sheep farmers it had a resurgence because another important market for our wool was Russia where they used it to make felt. The snow in Russia is so dry that the best boots are made of felt, and indeed those worn by soldiers are made out of wool that has been turned into felt. Any of you who've had a felted loden coat as I have, or a quilted hat will know how incredibly warm this material is. If you want to felt wool yourself, put it in the hot cycle of the washing machine. One of my neighbours made wonderful hats and purses and things, all of which she felted in her washing machine.

Wool in all its forms is perfectly easy to wash: if you want to put it in the washing machine, as I do, put it on the delicate cycle, not actually the wool cycle and it will come out beautifully. In New Zealand, they make fleeces of merino wool that you can put in the washing machine. There is every incentive to buy wool: it lasts longer, it keeps you warm and when you've finished with it, you can throw it on the fire and it'll keep you warm a little bit longer.

As is my wont, I seem to have meandered some distance from bio-diesel and alternative energy sources. I'm not particularly keen on wind power as found in these huge wind vanes that look like something out of a Magritte painting. The reason why is that if you look underneath them, you will find that they're supported by a cricket-pitch-sized concrete platform which seems to me not to be a good use of farming land. They're almost entirely made in Denmark and it's a fact that it's more expensive to repair them than to replace them. So if you go behind the first mountain range in southern Spain, you will see mile upon mile of rusting, rotting wind vanes, standing side by side with their new replacements. It's not an attractive sight and it makes you realise that perhaps the risk to your planet is greater than you think.

Wave power sounds like a good idea, although I don't know enough about it to decide either way. But there is one source of power, it seems to me, that is the most obvious and most usable and yet seems terribly neglected and that is solar energy. I remember fifty years ago, or certainly forty-five years ago, my friends the Colemans putting solar panels in their roof. These were the very early days of solar energy and the panels didn't work terribly wonderfully because it was a whole new concept then. Sadly, nowadays it still seems to work not terribly wonderfully because nobody has been giving it the attention it deserves. However, my interest in solar energy did give me reason to encounter the most splendid woman.

It's very seldom in one's life, or in my life, that one meets people one admires and respects but this was the year I met Annie Maw, who is the High Sheriff of Somerset. She is also paralysed from the waist down, having broken her back in a hunting accident when she was the master of the Mendip Farmers. She's a woman in her late fifties and you would have thought that following her accident being High Sheriff was quite enough, but not a bit of it. She was the guiding force behind what was known as the SolaRola adventure to raise money for Help for Heroes and other disabled charities.

The SolaRola team were five in number and included a girl who had won the paraplegic London Marathon and been placed on several other occasions (this is a wheelchair marathon), and two men, both of whom had broken their backs in accidents. The plan was to drive these SolaRolas, which were in fact the sort of golf buggy that President Bush used to go around in, only solar powered, from outside the Houses of Parliament to the Bath and West Show, over a period of about ten days to two weeks, planning to arrive at the show and be welcomed there. The solar-powered buggies were the invention of a remarkable man called Malcolm Moss who, having made a lot of money in the oil industry, had decided that the future lay in solar power and was now busy manufacturing solar-powered cells in Uttar Pradesh in India.

London to the Bath and West Showground is not a negligible journey even by car but the team were determined, regardless of the weather, to set off. It was John Gardiner, the political officer of the Countryside Alliance, a man I admire immensely for the quality of his brain, and who is married to the sculptress Olivia Musgrave, who persuaded me to be involved in the adventure. Not driving to Bath, obviously, but to speak at the dinner at their first night at Ham House and to be there to greet them at the Bath and West Show, where I was destined to be anyway.

I had met Annie and her husband Dickie, a general practitioner, beforehand at the house of a friend who was helping to organise the Hampshire/Wiltshire leg of the journey. Annie is good-looking, full of energy, humour and positive determination, with no sign of any form of self-pity, and who really did regard the journey as an adventure.

The day came and there they all were, assembled in their solar-powered wheelchair buggies outside the Houses of Parliament. My friend Annie Mallalieu, the Labour peer, was there together with various other people to see them off. They were accompanied by Robin Hanbury-Tennison, the explorer, on an electric motorbike. I was quite excited by the concept of this and I'm sure it'll be a great thing, but at the moment it's remarkably heavy and I wouldn't like to have to handle it. There was a distinct absence of Members of Parliament from any party to cheer them on, but the press were there and the television cameras and they duly set off on their journey. I saw them that night at Ham House where I spoke at the dinner and they were very buoyant and determined.

The weather in the ten days that followed was appalling. It rained heavily, there was a cold wind, the sort of days that one would have wanted to spend indoors, but I saw them again on the next leg of their adventure when they stopped for a barbecue in a barn in Hampshire and they were wet and cold and glad to get their food and just wanted to relax. That day they had taken a detour through the woods surrounding Windsor which had been very muddy and sticky and due to an organisational error they had found themselves on the main road as they came out of the woods. But they were nonetheless full of good spirits. The next time I saw them was down the line at the Bath and West Show, where they all arrived with Annie leading the way, still in fine fettle.

I had a go in one of the SolaRolas and it was a nifty little thing that whipped along at four miles an hour with the solar panels on the roof re-charging the battery. However on this trip, due to the inclement weather and the lack of sun, they had to be plugged in at night. Malcolm Moss assured me that the technology was there and there was no reason whatsoever why there shouldn't be a solar-powered car, travelling rather faster than four miles an hour. I did wonder why there wasn't such a car already and certainly why countries with much more sunlight than us aren't using this technology. I was delighted to have met Annie and Dickie and I have to say that I've acquired a new heroine in my life and let's only hope that the friendship continues.

My late brother Anthony, who lost his legs and was confined to a wheelchair, used to whizz around in his and had the kitchen designed in such a way that he could continue to cook and I must say I found this quite amazing. Yet a lot of people seem to find huge reserves of strength to help them to deal with the problems resulting from their situation.

My next engagement was at the first of the West Country shows that my friend in the coursing community, Mike Robinson, had suggested I might like to attend this year and that in so doing I might represent coursing in an area where not much is known about it. It was some years since I had last been to the West Country shows so I agreed and was put in touch with a remarkable woman called Alison Hawes who is the area representative for the Countryside Alliance down there and also their press officer, in a part of the country where there has been a number of hunting prosecutions.

At the time of writing, the Court of Appeal has just, and in my opinion quite rightly, found in favour of Tony Wright, the huntsman of the Exmoor Foxhounds who was prosecuted on videotape evidence provided by the League Against Cruel Sports, a misnamed organisation if ever there was one. The case originally came up before a magistrate who declared an interest in the case as he'd worked for the League on previous occasions.

Why at that point the Countryside Alliance lawyer didn't ask him to recuse himself is something I shall never understand, and unsurprisingly the magistrate found in favour of the prosecution.

It was then appealed to Judge Cottle, sitting in the Crown Court, who dismissed the conviction against Tony Wright in no uncertain terms. The League had tried to get rid of Judge Cottle from the case, saying that he had once hosted a meet at his home, which made Judge Cottle furious since he had never done any such thing and had no known association with hunting or field sports. The Crown Prosecution Service appealed Judge Cottle's judgement, asking him to give his reasons for his judgement, or state a case, which he refused to do, saying that this was a ridiculous prosecution that should never have been brought in the first place. It then went to the Court of Appeal who directed that Judge Cottle should state a case so that it could be considered if they found in favour of the LACS application. In the event the Court of Appeal sided with Judge Cottle and declared quite rightly that the burden of proof under the Hunting Act was on the prosecution. It is one of the prime principles of English law that the burden of proof is on the prosecution. This particular government has mucked around with our laws quite enough without starting to undo quite such an important piece of precedent.

When you consider that during the credit crisis this government seized the assets of the country of Iceland, under a piece of legislation that we'd been assured was only designed to deal with terrorists, and held them until such time as the British debts that could be paid were paid, it is worth noting that it is very dangerous to implement legislation that once on the statute books can be used for anything. I should think that when the next Conservative government comes in, we're going to have to spend quite an amount of time undoing all the bad law that Mr Blair and subsequently Mr Brown have imposed upon us. They whittled away at our historic freedoms in a terrifying fashion. Let me give you an example: it used to be the case that if you were locked up you could apply for bail with monotonous regularity and obviously if you were unsuccessful you stayed locked up. It is now the case that you have only the one bite, so if you're remanded in custody you can then appeal to a judge to grant you bail. But only on one single occasion (unless something terribly dramatic happens in the meantime). If it's refused, you stay there until your trial which can take many months or maybe even years. The right to bail and the implementation of the Habeas Corpus Acts were two of the most brilliant blows for liberty in legal systems anywhere.

You may well have read, so I must touch on it now, that I am pending prosecution for an alleged illegal coursing event. There are four counts: two suggest that I was hunting under the Hunting Act, under which coursing is also banned, and the others that I was attending illegal events. I pleaded not guilty to all the charges. My co-defendant is Mark Prescott, a great racehorse trainer and sporting baronet, who has done likewise. This, I would point out, is not a police prosecution against us, but has been brought by the International Fund for Animal Welfare, under the auspices of a very unpleasant man indeed called Joseph Hashman, who has long been a thorn in the side of the hunting community. If this case ever comes to court it will be interesting to come face to face with Mr Hashman. I may have seen him before, shouting abuse at me somewhere in the world.

There is also a police prosecution pending over the same alleged matter which involves two Yorkshire landowners, one of whom is the former racehorse trainer Peter Easterby and the other a former prominent and decorated member of Her Majesty's armed forces. It also involves the greyhound trainer Jackie Teal and, rather curiously, a very nice woman who has a pub called the Creswell Arms where various people who attended the alleged illegal event had breakfast on the morning of that day. I have subsequently stayed occasionally at the Creswell Arms, while attending a lure meeting in Yorkshire, and met the woman in question who knew nothing about coursing, had never been to a coursing meeting and whose only involvement with dogs was a very beautiful young bull mastiff who I don't think would have caught many hares. I think it's quite preposterous. And the only benefit that seems to have come out of it is that I now know a very nice, comfortable pub with delicious food where I shall be able to stay on future visits to Yorkshire.

The only end result the Hunting Act seems to have achieved is to provide a licence for various organisations that are against field sports to take on a vigilante role. There was recently a case in East Anglia brought against two eighty-year-olds by the RSPCA for alleged illegal coursing. Well, regardless of what the pair may or may not have been doing, it is my understanding that the RSPCA does not have a remit that covers wild animals. They are there to save abused dogs, donkeys, horses. Yet you try getting them out if you see neglected horses in a field; two nuns of my acquaintance rang them repeatedly to report horses who were chewing the bark of trees because they had no food and no water and the RSPCA did nothing.

Anyway, to return to the shows, Alison Hawes was a tower of strength. I have over the years, both on my own and with Johnny Scott, attended a number of game fairs and country fairs around the UK and we're welcomed both by the British Association for Shooting and Conservation (BASC) and by the Countryside Alliance to sit on their stands and sign books and talk to people and this is regarded as a good draw for whichever organisation's stand we happen to be on. I find it a great pleasure to get out into the countryside, to meet like-minded people, to talk to them and to visit the food stands as well – there's always a food stand in any show – to see what people are doing and if there are any products or innovations that one particularly approves of. I also like to see all the producers of fishing rods, creels, ferreting nets and other sorts of useful things that you can't just go into a general store and buy.

The first of the West Country shows I went to was the Royal Devon County Show, which is held on a permanent showground just outside Exeter. On my previous visit, about three years before, when I attended the show with Johnny, we had stayed at a very nice bed and breakfast owned by some people called Thompson, which is only ten minutes from the showground and I was fortunate enough to be able to obtain a bed there again. Alison had organised everything to perfection so that I didn't have to cart hundreds of books around on the day of the show, or the night before, as was usually the case, which was a delight. All I had to do was get into my car, turn up and make sure I had a pen.

She'd also organised a disability scooter for me. I have a metal plate in my instep, as a result of a riding accident when I was eleven and I'm afraid that too many years of disco dancing in unsuitable shoes – oh yes, I was a great little mover once – and marching for miles on hard streets at Countryside Alliance rallies, and of course too much weight and the general wear and tear of life have left their mark; and cooks spend a lot of time on their feet, as do barristers. I remember the late Sir Leonard Caplan QC saying to me once, in my very early days of practice, 'Whatever you do, Clarissa, look after your feet!' Sadly I didn't take his advice so my foot causes me quite a lot of discomfort now and makes me rather slow and lame.

As these country shows cover quite a large area I was very thankful that Alison had provided me with a scooter, since it meant I could nip round to the different platforms that I was supposed to be sitting on talking about various matters and also go to the food and other tents without too much trouble or having to bother the show organisers for a car to get me there. The scooter gave me an enormous amount of freedom and it was really quite a nippy little thing.

Any specialists I have consulted over whether I can have a replacement plate have said cheerily, 'You just better hope that the IRA start shooting people through the instep rather than the knee-cap.' I understand that most of the research on restoring and repairing knee-caps was done in Belfast where of course the IRA generously provided the medics with a surplus of knee-caps to operate on. It's amazing how wars and violence lead to so many innovations in medicine and surgery in general.

White Pit

This is a rather curious milk pudding found over in the Gloucestershire/Somerset borders. Despite the name it's very nice. Especially nice if it's made with proper milk. Even better if it's made with unpasteurised milk, but perfect with Prosperous milk.

½lb (225g) butter
3oz (75g) flour
2 pints (1.2 litres) warm milk
½ pint (300ml) black treacle
4 eggs
½ teaspoon ground cinnamon

Preheat the oven to 180°C/350°F/gas mark 4. Melt half the butter, stir in the flour and gradually add the milk. Stir continuously until the mixture has thickened and is smooth. Bring to the boil and simmer for a few minutes and remove from the heat. Stir in the treacle and add the eggs. Leave to cool. The mixture should now be cold and when baked it will separate into a jelly at the base and custard at the top. Pour the mixture into a 4½-pint (2.7-litre), greased pie dish, dot with the remaining butter and sprinkle with cinnamon. Bake in the oven for 1 hour. Allow to cool and serve cold.

May

Lay your face in the May morning dew
And true love will come to you

It's the month of May and the minds of fishing people turn to the mayfly season. The mayfly lives, loves and dances for only one single day. However its existence for this brief period has an enormous impact on fishing in the chalkstreams and in particular in the Test Valley and its tributaries. This capillary of rivers has long been regarded as the promised land of chalkstream trout fishing. Chalkstream fishing is not like ordinary fishing, but is basically about stalking the trout, best of all the wild trout.

The water, if the river is properly kept, is gin clear so that the trout can see you long before you see it, unless you are very careful and clever and watch where your shadow is cast, where the light is coming from and how you can cast a fly on to the fish's nose where it wants to eat it, without the fish being alerted by any movement from you, your rod, or your line. Good trout rods cost many hundreds of pounds and many books have been written on the subject, not just of fly-fishing but of fly-fishing in chalkstreams. Mayflies occur in most chalkstreams, but in much smaller numbers than they do on the Test and its tributaries. It is a magical thing to see the mayflies dance: they hatch and rise up in a spiral, swirling together around a tree or other tall plant; then they mate and lay their eggs and they die. Sometimes dazzled by the sun's reflection off a car windscreen, or even the bodywork if the car's the right colour, they may mistake it for water and die there. But when they die over the river, the trout go mad in a feeding frenzy, leaping out of the river, performing perfect somersaults, and returning to the river with a mouthful of mayfly. They are hungry from the winter and the coolness of spring up until then and the absence of fly life. Those of you who fish will know that what you look for when you're fishing is to match the fly you put on to your line to whatever is hatching at the time.

The native British trout is the brown trout, which tastes delicious, is a wary and clever fish to stalk and thrives well on the wildlife of the rivers. Like the grey squirrel, there is an incomer in our waters which is the rainbow trout, to my mind a floppy, not very tasty fish that will put up a good fight but doesn't really belong here and is taking up space that could otherwise be utilised by wild fish, or by wild trout at least.

The regulation of the Test and its tributaries is carried out under the auspices of the Test Valley Association. The river weed is only allowed to be cut within certain dates; this is partly to hold water within the river and to make sure that the fishing isn't affected by quantities of reed floating through from your neighbour's weed-cut at a time when you're not expecting it and when it will interfere with your fishing. The weed floats on down the river, picking up weed from further beats and finally comes to rest against a huge barricade where it is lifted out of the river and dried and used for various industries, including thatching.

To obtain a rod on a beat on the Test Valley is very much stepping into dead men's shoes. It's not something people give up lightly having acquired one and, although it is expensive, is regarded as well worth the investment. Historically, the doyen of beats was that occupied by the Houghton Club which has pontificated on all matters of chalkstream trout fishing for quite a long time and its members in their club room, overlooking the high street in the charming town of Stockbridge, have regarded themselves as infinitely superior in these matters. There is, however, a canker on the face of Eden, in that they're advocating the triploid scheme. To ensure a good supply of fish on fishing beats, in many instances the hen fish are caught up after they have mated and stripped of their eggs which are then hatched in incubators and returned to the river of their mother's birth. In some cases the fish are sold to other areas but the best practice is to return the fry to the river into which they would have been born. The triploid scheme involves heating the eggs of the fish as you are hatching them so that they are born sterile. As a result rainbow trout have been added to the Houghton water, something that would never have been tolerated in the past, but the treatment will supposedly stop them mating with wild fish and polluting the strain. To my mind it seems more about a short cut to overstocking.

Size, as in everything in any male-dominated world, matters and people are looking for bigger fish to put in their game books. However, what do I know? If you really want to find out more about the whole question of chalkstream fishing and fishing in the Test Valley and its tributaries, I recommend you to a very good blog called testvalleyriverkeeper.blogspot. com, written by Chris de Cani, who is a keeper of one of the tributaries of the Test.

I have fished only intermittently throughout my life, largely because I have had neither the money nor the access and in my early days it was probably just as well since I might have been found floating cold and dead down the salmon river. In my drinking years, I was not in any fit state to cast a line, let alone wade into a river. And nowadays, I'm much too busy. The one thing about fishing, like anything in this life and certainly any field sport, is the amount of practice involved; the more you fish, the better you get at it, just as the more you shoot, the better you get at it. I simply don't have that time.

I suspect that my wading days are over, if not only because when I had a burglary in my house during a period when I was away, one of the few things they stole was my fishing waders. Now these were chest waders. I had quite a lot of trouble getting chest waders that fitted me and I can't quite understand why the skinny junkie and his friend who broke into my house were in any way interested in waders that would probably have gone three times round both of them together. What is more bizarre is that they didn't steal the felt-soled wading boots that went with them. I have visions in the small hours of the morning of some sort of fantasist who had commissioned them to come and steal my fishing waders so that he could lie wrapped in rubber and think of me . . . but I suspect that's just my idle thoughts.

The last time I went salmon fishing was a few years ago on the Murthly beat at Dunkeld on the River Tay. That is the beat in which Miss Ballantine caught her record-breaking salmon in 1922, which still holds the record. I was interested to discover that in fact she caught it while trolling from a boat, which is a technique where you trail the bait in the water behind the boat and not on a cast fly. And furthermore that after playing the fish for some time, it went between two rocks where her father, who was the ghillie on that particular beat of the river, went in with a gaff, or long-handled hook, something you're not allowed to do nowadays, and hauled out the fish. I don't say this to diminish Miss Ballantine, but to remark that when doing the self-same thing I also hooked a very large fish which I played for a prolonged period of time, until it too went between two rocks and I had to let it go. I consoled myself with the thought that I don't have the wall space for a stuffed sixty-pound salmon and nor do I have a cooker or a pan big enough to have cooked it.

In salmon fishing, it is a rule that you release the first fish you catch and then you're allowed to take the next one home. If you're fishing in the autumn of course it may be a red run fish, one that has spawned and is reaching the end of its days, in which case all you could possibly do is smoke it. Much the same applies to trout fishing in that you are allowed two fish on any given fishing day and you have to put the others back. I have always found this rule deeply disappointing as I never catch even the first salmon so how would I ever get to take one home?

One of my more fascinating experiences of fishing was haaf-netting on the Nith which is a tributary of the Solway. Haaf-netting is the ancient Viking method of fishing where you stand in the water up to your oxters, which is all right now in these days of nice warm waders, but God help the poor old Vikings holding this net which is made out of cedar wood which floats and is in the form of a cross of Lorraine if you like, with the net suspended between the two arms of the cross. It's rather like wild-fowling in that you have to know the paths of the salmon in the water. I thought it would be desperately boring but in fact it was utterly fascinating. You see the river from a different angle because you're practically at eye level with the fish and when the fish comes towards you it's at what seems like the pace of a torpedo; you can see it quite clearly heading straight for you, and it's pretty unnerving.

We were filming haaf–netting for *Clarissa and the Countryman*. I caught the only round fish of the day, but it was a rather large grey mullet, which is not the same as catching a salmon, while Johnny just got a couple of flounders. When the fish comes into your net, you have to lift the net up and over so that the fish is trapped in it and you then return to the shore, towing your net and your fish in order to despatch the fish, or else you release it. You stand in a line with your fellow fishermen and as the tide comes in or indeed out, the person at the affected end moves to the other end so that when you think you're going to drown, you move in and start again nearer the shore or vice versa if the tide is going out. I thoroughly enjoyed it. The fact that it was a particularly beautiful day might have had something to do with it as well.

Haaf–netting is now more or less obsolete on most rivers because it's done individually and should not be equated with netting which is a case of leaving nets in and waiting for the salmon. We also filmed fishing on the Bann, one of the great fishing rivers in Northern Ireland. The weir there, which was installed to catch the salmon coming up, had what was known as the King's Gap through which a limited number of fish were able to escape the weir and go upriver to spawn. The Bann, as late as the 1960s, was fishing out thousands of tonnes of salmon which were then sold to the London markets.

The thing to remember about a running salmon is that it is not thinking of eating, but snaps at your fly or your lure because it's irritated by it, so when you're fishing for salmon you have to be very accurate. Wild salmon numbers have been badly affected by the netting of salmon at sea and one can only commend the efforts of the North Atlantic Salmon Trust to persuade people not to practise this. It's one of those curious facts that the salmon on a fishmonger's slab is worth £3-plus per pound whereas a fish that is caught for sport is worth several thousand pounds to the area, not just in jobs and equipment but also in expenditure in hotels, fishing lodges and ancillary shopping and so is therefore something to be much encouraged. Those organisations such as PETA, who want to ban fishing as well as everything else in the line of field sports or indeed animal cultivation, call it 'the forgotten blood sport'. If you go on their Internet site, you will see how strongly they wish to abolish it.

This takes me back by a circuitous route to the West Country shows because it was at the Royal Bath and West, my second show in the area, that I decided to order myself a split cane fishing rod from a nice young man working out of Devon. I don't imagine that I will fish any better with a split cane rod, it's simply that I like old-fashioned things. Modern rods are of carbon fibre or very light metal. In my kitchen most of the kitchen implements date from before the First World War, if not even earlier; my only acknowledgements to modernity are my Run pans and my Magimix.

The Bath and West Show was quite different from the Royal Devon, being much bigger and less agricultural. I found myself staying in an extremely nice bed and breakfast which occupied what had been the stable block of an early nineteenth-century house with the river running through the grounds. At breakfast I met a woman who supplied animal soaps and lotions to stop itching, and by herbal and holistic means treated skin defects in any animal from horses to dogs. The terrier who lives where I do, Archie, gets allergies to pollen in the summer and itches like mad and I'm happy to relate that the soap was most efficacious.

Also staying there, and rather more exciting for me, was a young woman whose husband was a barrister and who was making jams and pickles and chutneys and so forth and was, for some reason, situated in the bee tent rather than the food tent at the show. I'm always slightly dubious about people who make these sorts of tracklements because most of the time they don't taste terribly good. They're beautifully packaged and well marketed but when you come to eat them they're either too sweet or too bland.

However, I was determined to go to the bee tent to visit Victoria Cranfield, the young woman in question. The bee tent itself was extremely interesting because it had all sorts of information on apiculture in general, on different types of hives for keeping them in, and on bee viruses that are making the rounds at the moment, and although I knew quite a lot of this, it was very well set out. When I found my friend, there she was at her stand with all sorts of diverse accompaniments, and I tasted my way through them. As a result I gave her a quote which she's since put on her website saying, 'The finest jams, chutneys and pickles I have ever eaten'. They ranged from bitter orange marmalade to a very good home-made lime pickle, through rowan jellies, elderberry jellies and all kinds of other delights. I do recommend her products to you and no doubt you'll be able to order them from her website or indeed find her at whichever of the country shows she attends. The company name was Cranfield's Foods.

I then went on to the food tent and in contrast to the one in Devon where there really was nothing much of interest, the one here was marvellous. I'm very keen on domestic salt production, since it seems to me ridiculous that we should pay huge sums of money to buy imported sea salt from France when we're more than capable of producing our own. Maldon sea salt from Essex is perhaps the best known, but when Jennifer and I were filming *Two Fat Ladies*, we succeeded in accidentally promoting Halen Mon which is a very good Welsh sea salt that is now doing better than ever. For a number of years I've been trying to persuade some people who make Cornish sea salt to sell it commercially and I came across them at the Bath and West Show. Their Cornish sea salt is now beautifully packaged and I recommend it to you.

On another stand I found salamis of all different shapes and sizes made from local Devon meat. These were excellent, some of them flavoured with fennel, some of them with chilli. Once again, salamis are a product I'm always rather dubious about because they never live up to their promise, but these were extremely good and by dint of the fact that I'd left a couple of them in a friend's larder by accident, I know that they also keep terribly well.

There was a rather charming stand called Cake in a Box selling cakes cooked in wooden boxes. You buy your box and a fruitcake – I took mine back to the Countryside Alliance stand where I was based, and we all had it for tea and it was very good – but afterwards you keep the box and continue to bake your own cakes either to your own fruitcake mixture following their instructions or to the recipe they give you. I thought this was a delightful idea, and of course historically cakes used to be baked in wooden boxes because metalwork didn't become available until after the Industrial Revolution.

The food at these shows is usually pretty dreadful. The organisers make large sums of money from selling the commercial hamburger of the more horrible type. They charge their purveyors large entry fees, and take the money rather than encourage local producers and people who are making home-made hamburgers out of the good four quarters of the meat, which is a much healthier option. When Jamie Oliver was supposedly teaching children to eat healthily, I could never understand why he kept trying to feed them salads. Surely the object should have been to feed them a proper hamburger and a proper sausage to persuade them away from the revolting variety.

Nor is it clear to me why salad, like chicken, is supposed to be the healthy option for a meal. The amount of chlorine gas that you find in packets of salad is so great that if Saddam Hussein had said he was setting up a salad plant, he'd probably have got away with his chlorine gas production. Salad isn't healthy; it's nothing, just water at best and as most of it is grown hydroponically with chemicals and packed with chlorine, I cannot fathom why it should be regarded as healthy. And now we are bombarded by this wonderful notion that we must have five different portions of fruit and vegetables a day, excluding potatoes. Yet the Irish nation survived extremely well, historically, on the potato. It was the failure of the potato crop rather than the potato as a nutritional vegetable that was the problem. And why we need to consume five different ones? I mean, I could understand if perhaps you had two fruit and three vegetables or three fruit and two vegetables, but why does it have to be different ones? Once again, it seems to me to be a government directive to try to promote the supermarkets who sell all these peculiar types of fruit and vegetables.

In any event, one of the dishes I particularly like to eat in the West Country is the Cornish pasty. Commercial Cornish pasties are made quite wrongly with minced meat and carrots. The meat for proper Cornish pasties is chopped, not minced, which I assume is used for cheapness and speed, and the chopped meat makes it a much nicer dish. Heaven knows why they add carrot because there is a good reason for its absence in a real Cornish pasty. (And, as some of you may know, I'm averse to carrot, but that's another matter.) Historically, in England the carrot flies hatch twice a year, and you grow your carrot crop between those two hatchings. In Cornwall, presumably because of the milder climate, carrot flies are around all the time so carrots were not grown beyond the Tamar and therefore were not used in any Cornish dishes. The quality of the Cornish pasties at the Bath and West Show was terrific, both in the food tent where they were quite delicious and indeed on stands around the site.

The great delight of being on the Countryside Alliance stand or in the Countryside area is the presence of all the different hound packs. It's quite common to have foxhounds, harriers, beagles and, at the Bath and West Show, the Devon and Cornwall Mink Hounds, who were there on this occasion. Those of you who watched *Clarissa and the Countryman* will perhaps remember the magic occasion when we went hunting on the Tamar with them and their handsome young huntsman, Mark Prout. He used to erect barns for a living and went to the first Hyde Park countryside rally where he met one of the great doyennes of hunting and was encouraged to take it up. Since then he has taken over the Devon and Cornwall Mink Hounds and made a huge success of it.

The mink hounds are the old stock that were the otter hounds before otter hunting was banned and they were transferred to hunting mink. The mink is an unpleasant animal that even the most devoted fluffy bunny brigader would find difficulty in loving. It kills for pleasure and is almost impossible to kill without using hounds because it will not take dead bait, but is only interested in killing live creatures. When I was working on a pheasant shoot some minks got into a farm near us and took out 2,000 pheasant poults in one night, just taking their heads off and leaving them for dead.

You may remember a few years ago when the antis released a number of mink from a fur farm into the countryside. These ran amuck, killing everything in sight and heavily contributing to the demise of the water vole of which there aren't very many anyway. The water vole is what I grew up calling a water rat and is of course Ratty in *The Wind in the Willows*, but for some politically correct reason they are now called water voles. The minks then developed distemper which spread to the otter population and also, I understand, to the water shrew population, knocking back both those species. On one occasion the minks even bit a baby in its pram. However, for the moment they seem to have been cut back by their own distemper.

Anyway, we filmed Mark Prout hunting his wonderful, hairy mink/otter hounds through the river, following the scent of the mink. Otter hounds, by reason of the habitat of their historic prey, have a very long nose and will hunt a scent that is perhaps a week old until they find their quarry. Mark Prout is now a married father of two and carrying rather more condition than he did when we filmed with him, but it was delightful to see him again and he was as charming and positive as ever. As Jorrocks says, 'Show me a man as hunts and I loves him already.' So it is always a pleasure to be surrounded by like-minded people.

Health and Safety have decided that if hounds are on show and allowed to be handled and fondled by children, and they have been ever since I can remember, there must be wet-wipes present so that the children can de-contaminate themselves after touching the dogs. At this show, a very disagreeable woman came up to me. One of the disadvantages of sitting in a public place is you do get one or two unpleasant incidents, although most of the time it's totally delightful. Anyway, this woman came up to me and said, looking at the beagles, which are of course quite small, 'Are those hound puppies?' I said, 'No, madam, they're beagles.' 'Oh,' she said, 'are they for sale?' And I said, 'No, madam, they're for huntsmen to take into the ring to display, so that the huntsmen can answer questions about the nature of the beagle and what their quarry is historically and what they do now.' 'Oh,' she said, 'well, I'm very glad to see that they're handing out wet-wipes when people are stroking those nasty, dirty dogs.' Then rather to my surprise she said, 'I'm a great admirer of what you do in the food world.' Next, having made it quite clear she thought hunting should continue to be banned, she said, 'May I shake your hand?' And I simply couldn't resist it. I looked her straight in the eye and said, 'Not until you've passed me the wet-wipes.' At which point she walked off in a huff, much to the amusement of the people who were clustering around my table.

Journalists often say to me, 'Of course hunting is carrying on exactly the same as ever, isn't it?' And I say to them, 'How on earth would I know?' They ask, 'What do you mean?' And I say, 'Well, I'm a fat, old cook, and even if I were on a horse, the chances of my being up front with the huntsmen and the hounds and finding out what was going on would be absolutely zilch, so I really don't know.' Which is of course the truth. I know that there are more people who support hunting and the repeal of the ban than there ever were before the ban and I look forward to the day when everything is returned to the norm. This naturally requires a change of government because the Labour government are never going to admit that they were wrong and of course – what price New Labour? – Kier Hardy's two tenets were the abolition of fox-hunting and the House of Lords.

It strikes me with overwhelming horror every time I think about it that the quid pro quo that Tony Blair threw his backbenchers to allow them to use the Parliament Act on the Hunting Bill was to get them to endorse the war in Iraq. I don't have a very high opinion of politicians, I don't have a very high opinion of Labour politicians in particular, and I don't have any regard at all for Mr Blair or Mr Brown or any of their ilk, but even I wouldn't have thought they would be quite so cynical and that this appalling war should have been bought off the back of a centuries-old field sport. If the government had offered MPs something in the way of education, say the return of the student maintenance grant or the return of the polytechnic or something to do with health or social benefit, I might just have understood it, even if I didn't approve of it, but to join America for reasons that really only involve oil beggars belief.

The Bath and West is a four-day show – that is a very long show indeed, especially if you're taking part in it – and is noted for being subject to bad weather. This year was no exception. Fortunately the SolaRolas had arrived before then to a great welcome at the end of their journey from London and they exchanged cheques and received messages of goodwill from all sorts of people including the Prince of Wales, and showed off their prowess on their SolaRolas, although they looked quite exhausted. But at the end of the second day, the heavens opened and the whole place was awash. It was known as the Bath and West Tsunami when something like four inches of rain fell in forty minutes just as we were all about to go home, and getting out of the showground was more than a little difficult as there was a blocked drain. Why is there always a blocked drain? Wherever you go when there's heavy rain there's always a blocked drain, isn't there? And so the road out of the showground flooded. I was lucky, I got out early but a lot of people were stuck there for a long time.

I was really rather surprised that Health and Safety didn't close down the rest of the show. The ground was incredibly wet, and here we had another brilliant example of Health and Safety at work. They went to the stall of a man who was selling wellington boots and outdoor clothes, who had put down straw that he'd obtained from the show, because his stand was just a puddle. This was obviously to soak up the water and give people something to stand on and they said, 'You can't do that.' He said, 'Why not?' And they said, 'It's a hazard and might catch fire.' Not surprisingly he lost his temper, whipped out a box of matches and said, 'A thousand pounds to anybody who manages to set fire to that straw' – and they did slink away rather shamefacedly.

Moroccan Trout

May is mayfly month when you go out and catch lots of trout. There is nothing nicer than a brown trout straight out of the river but after a while one gets a little tired of just having it plain cooked so here is a Moroccan suggestion for what you might do or more especially what you might do with a rainbow trout if that's what you've been catching because they really don't taste of anything very much. You can prepare the packets of fish that you are going to cook on your barbecue in advance and keep them in the refrigerator and they will in fact improve with being in the marinade for that much longer.

4 trout or the fillets of 4 trout
1 preserved lemon
4 tablespoons thinly sliced spring onion
2 small cloves of garlic, peeled and finely chopped
2 tablespoons each chopped green coriander
and flat-leafed Italian parsley
2 tablespoons olive oil
2 tablespoons lemon juice
4 pinches each per fish of hot red
pepper and powdered saffron
salt and freshly ground black pepper

Place the fish or fillets on individual sheets of aluminium foil. If you are using fillets, put two together on one sheet. Cut the preserved lemon into eight thin wedges. Place two wedges on each fillet and sprinkle with the spring onion, garlic, coriander and parsley. In a bowl, combine the olive oil, lemon juice, hot red pepper and saffron, slightly softened in a little warmed water, and pour over the fish fillets. Season with salt and pepper to taste. Fold the foil and seal securely. Place the packets on the grid of a charcoal grill, about eight inches above the heat, or in an oven preheated to 180°C/350°F/gas mark 4. Cook for 20 minutes and serve immediately.

June

A swarm of bees in May is worth a load of hay,
A swarm of bees in June is worth a silver spoon,
A swarm of bees in July isn't worth a fly

I managed to get home for about four days at the beginning of June to deal with my tax inspection. Maybe it's because I'm one of the very few celebrities who actually lives in Scotland, or because I'm usually too busy to remember to file the tax returns on time but I seem to have quite a few tax inspections. Or perhaps because, despite my entitlement to a passport, I am theoretically a white settler. In other words, somebody born in England, living across the Scottish border. The Scots are the most tolerant of people when it comes to accepting foreigners in their midst, although this does not particularly apply to the English and I have to work quite hard to reassure them that, despite my accent, I have enough Scottish blood in my genes to be allowed to live here. So far, I've always come out of inspections smelling of roses because I really don't have the time to dream up schemes for defrauding the Inland Revenue. Like most people, I suppose, I resent paying taxes, especially to this government. In particular, I resent paying for the wars in Iraq and in Afghanistan. The war in Iraq should never have happened; it was a con trick based entirely on false premises, and the war in Afghanistan was just a waste of time; people don't win in Afghanistan.

I remember seeing a parade in Kabul just before the Russians pulled out and at the back was a large banner, obviously aimed at European television as it was in English and it said, 'Afghanistan, conqueror of Empires' and that's so right. The last English incursion was forced to abandon the garrison under Lord Elphinstone at Kabul in 1842, and while attempting to reach the safety of Jalalabad the troops were annihilated by Afghan forces. Only one man survived. He was a colour sergeant and they saved him because he was very brave and sent him back as a warning to the rest. And every time I hear on the radio that yet another soldier has died in Afghanistan, that comes back to me.

As I was driving around I heard a senior member of the medical profession on the radio who said that we could buy the whole of the Afghanistan poppy crop for what it cost to keep our troops in the country for three weeks. The health service needs opium, it needs morphine, which is a derivative of opium, for painkillers and pain relief for people with terminal illnesses; it even presumably needs heroin. How much simpler it would be just to buy it and use it legally. It would keep it off the streets and it would save an awful lot of lives both among the army and over here.

This particular inspection, however, was slightly irritating because it had come about due to the failure of my trustees in bankruptcy, at the time when I was bankrupt, to file any tax returns. The Inland Revenue had, under the Blair government, struck a deal with the five largest accountants/insolvency practitioners in the country and all the revenues went to them. These companies may not only be the largest, they're also of course the most expensive, so that the creditor doesn't particularly benefit at all. In my case, although I paid over a fairly substantial part of my income to my trustee, none of it made its way to the creditor, the Inland Revenue. Tax inspectors are by and large rather reasonable and nice people and once the inspector realised that I was not about to go bankrupt again and did actually have the money to pay the outstanding taxes, we all got along quite swimmingly. So, between an extremely nice Revenue inspector and my excellent accountants, we sorted out the problems and I went off again.

My third of the West Country shows was the Royal Cornwall, which was a delightful show, not terribly big by comparison to the other two, but full of charm and enthusiasm and the great benefit to me was that the bed and breakfast I was staying in was precisely halfway between the showground and Padstow. Padstow, as you will know, is where Rick Stein has based himself and I decided to take myself off to eat in his restaurant. When I arrived, I hadn't booked but they were able to give me a seat at the bar and I enjoyed myself eating some very good oysters with spicy sausages and some excellent sushi. In fact I enjoyed the experience so much, I went back the next two nights as well. It's rare that I would do this at any eating establishment so it was a great tribute to Rick.

When I first met him, he was Richard Stein and had just written his excellent first book, *English Seafood Cookery*, which won the Glenfiddich Prize. I remember having great amusement with it because it contained a recipe for anchovy ice cream. At the time I was working in Books for Cooks in Notting Hill and I sold a lot of copies of the book and used to try to persuade people to make the anchovy ice cream and bring it back to me to try, but nobody ever did so eventually I had to make it myself and very good it was too. Although he has written many books since, some of them glamorous and full of pictures, and some of them from exotic foreign places, this is still the book of his that I return to most frequently. When I visited the restaurant

Rick was not there, sadly, but in Australia. However his head chef came and talked to me, and said that he'd emailed Rick who had sent me his good wishes and as he couldn't give me a drink on the house, because I don't drink, he'd given me a free course, so I got my starter for nothing. I was so impressed that, as you will hear, I returned later in the year.

I do recommend it to you. People will say it's expensive, although I didn't find it so, but it's worth every penny. The staff are charming and efficient and the food is sensational. The quality of the fish is second to none. It is not often that I'm able to compliment so happily what are now called celebrity chefs; most of them actually get a lot worse after they appear on television. There was a time when I used to save all my pennies to go and eat Gary Rhodes's food when he was running the restaurant in Hill Street, the Greenhouse, but now I find that his restaurants have become formulaic. Certainly the one that opened and closed in Edinburgh, with the best will in the world, was not one that I would rush to eat in.

I know from my own experience how difficult it is to run a restaurant long-distance and to have to trust one's chef to make sure everything is up to the standards one has set. Rick Stein is one of the few who has managed to achieve it. I only went to the main restaurant because my feet were sore at the end of a long day at the show and it was handy for the car park, but my godson tells me that the fish and chips at the fish and chip shop are extremely good, if somewhat expensive.

I went across to Padstow with a friend another time to Rick Stein's and decided that we would have the Singapore crab, which was wonderfully messy but most delicious and scrumptious to taste. And I remembered that when I was going down to Cornwall to visit friends on the train in my drinking

With my friend Johnny Scott and some amiable chickens on the filming of *Clarissa and the Countryman* back in 2002.

I was very lucky to be invited to Sandringham to meet the
President of the WI . . . one of my heroes, the Queen!

Laying out a huge spread for the very special feast for *The King's Cookbook*, at Gainsborough Old Hall, February 2008.

Yet another book signing, this time at the
Royal Devon County Show, May 2008.

In the ring at the Royal Devon County Show with Mark Prout and his mink hounds – none were as beautiful as Kipper though.

At my favourite pub, the Cholmondeley Arms, in talks with the chef Dan Whitford over their 20th birthday menu, October 2008.

Kipper with a splendid fish he has landed.

My friend Sonic painted in her heyday.

days, because it was a very long journey I would go and collect a crab with black bean and chilli from a Chinese restaurant and take it and a bottle of hock and hop on to the train. I'd spread out a newspaper to catch the mess and spend the entire journey eating my crab. It's a very good way of not having people sitting opposite you, I can tell you. And I feel I need it even more so now. They say that you're growing old when you spend your time thinking how much better things were when you were young, and I dare say that may be right in a great many circumstances, but it's difficult to see how one can fail to think that much has gone downhill in this day and age. Take railway trains for instance.

I live in Scotland. Recently I found myself in London intending to travel home on the Saturday because I'd had to stay down to do a bit of extra work on the Friday. Imagine my horror when I discovered that on neither Saturday nor Sunday is there one single train from London, the capital of England, to Edinburgh, the capital of Scotland, that does not require you to change at least once, and in most cases two or three times, usually on to a bus for at least one stage of the journey. I did find one train that left St Pancras rather than King's Cross and you changed at Derby – possibly it's called the Bonnie Prince Charlie Memorial Journey – where you only had to wait about forty minutes and then you got on to a train that went straight to Edinburgh. That particular train left quite early in the morning and took well over six hours to make the journey.

Deciding that my temper wouldn't really tolerate a six- to seven-hour journey with intermittent changes, I resolved to stay an extra two nights in London which cost me roughly the same as the train fare. A first-class return train fare from London to Edinburgh or vice versa now costs you almost £400. If you book early, of course, and decide that you're going to travel at certain times, you will pay less, but if you want the spontaneity and freedom of travel, that's what it costs. You could fly most of the way round the world for less than that.

I remember coming up to London when I was seventeen. My mother had determined that I would learn to drive as soon as possible and had been economical with the truth to my headmistress, telling her that I had to come up from school because I needed some medical tests. Whereas in fact I was taking driving lessons. I used to travel on the Brighton Belle first thing in the morning and it was a delight. You got an excellent breakfast, the journey was about an hour, and you just had time to eat your porridge and kippers or whatever else you were having before you arrived in London. Now the railways have done away with dining cars because they say they are so heavy to pull that they use up too much fuel; and besides, they can put on extra carriages in their place. I have to say that it's quite a long time since I travelled on a train with a dining car in any event and since GNER lost its franchise for the east coast service, I haven't managed to find a single one that sells anything approaching edible food.

Some years ago a buffet steward on one of the southern lines was actually sacked because he was making cheese on toast, on his own initiative, for his passengers. This was on an evening train where there was no other food. It was very good cheese on toast I remember, too. Now all you get is rather horrible, un-constipating sandwiches, or if you want to order hot food from the in-seat dining menu there is nothing much to tempt you, or indeed safe to eat, although I dare say I'm wrong on the latter.

If you are on a Virgin train it's far worse because the seats aren't comfortable and the food is even more unpleasant. I once had a Virgin steward almost fling back in my face the small tip I had tried to give him for going off and getting me some ice. Quite clearly he didn't like to think that he was in a service industry. And why a train over the same distance from London to Edinburgh should now take half an hour longer than it did fifteen years ago is quite beyond me. Do you know that it takes longer to get to Grange-over-Sands from London by public transport today than it did by stagecoach? People say why don't you fly, but that has now become such an unpleasant experience that only the very young will really endure it and if it takes you twenty minutes to get to your gate once you've got through the non-existent security scanners, I'm probably likely to miss the plane, even without being stopped and asked for my autograph.

Once when I flew down from Scotland the woman who booked me in had given me one of those seats with more leg room in front of the emergency exit. Unfortunately she put me in the middle where the smaller seat meant I had to ask for an extension for my seatbelt. The rather unpleasant steward told me that I couldn't sit there because under the Civil Aviation Acts I was clinically obese and therefore would endanger use of the exit in the event of a crash. I asked him if he had a copy of that particular bit of that Aviation Act which of course he didn't, and he was extremely offensive until the rather large man sitting in the same seat on the other side of the aisle said, 'Well, I'm going to ask you for an extension; are you saying that I'm clinically obese?' At which point everybody fell about laughing and the steward retreated, hurt. The very large man in question was Matthew Pinsent, the rower. As I don't need an extension when I sit in an ordinary seat, I'm at a loss as to why one was necessary in that particular seat.

Is it, I wonder, really wrong on my part to expect service as good if not better than it was when I was young?

We had a lovely time, my friend and I, revisiting places from our respective childhoods and bits of our life. I used to go down to Cornwall with my family at Easter most years because my father took a rugby team there and in those days we used to stay at the Tregenna Castle in St Ives. My mother was always happy to go to Cornwall because her grandfather had been a Cornish tin mining engineer trained at the Cambourne School of Mines. When the Cornish tin mining industry began to fail because of the fickleness of the seams and the difficulty in following them, he went out to Australia and subsequently to Malaysia for the tin.

When I was young, coal mining was commonplace in Britain. We were a nation that ran on coal and all over Britain, not just in the Welsh valleys, there were huge areas that relied entirely on the coal mining industry. Then came the Thatcher years, when the unions decided they were going to hold the country to ransom and Mrs Thatcher decided that she was going to destroy the miners; inevitably the ordinary people in the mining communities got caught in the middle.

I remember going out to collect money and raise funds for children in the mining communities who quite literally had no shoes, not much food and in some areas were on the verge of starvation. I always found this rather perplexing as the miners' union had huge sums of money which they were busy hiding offshore so that the Thatcher government couldn't get their hands on it. And nobody in the social services seemed to see fit to do something to help these children. The end result was, as it always is, that the ordinary people suffered and whole families were divided by the question of whether it had been right to go back to work and be labelled a 'scab' or to let your children starve. It is certainly true that nobody canvassing for the Conservative Party need bother going into those areas; a parrot under a Labour hat would get more votes. And there remain large areas of the country where the economy has never recovered and there are simply no jobs available.

This at a time when fossil fuels are running out but we have enough coal to keep us going for the next 300 years and I would have thought that it was not beyond the imagination of scientists to find some way to burn coal without causing problems with carbon emissions. I gather that the increase in the price of base metals has made it feasible for at least one Cornish tin mine to open up again and mine tin. Wheal Jane is the best known of the old tin mines, with its seam running under the sea and interestingly they were taking tin from it as early as the nineteenth century. Today it is a centre of expertise in mining and minerals. And it would be quite nice to think in the days when the travellers are back to stealing lead off church roofs because lead has soared in value that the lead mines that so tempted the Romans could be opened up again.

When the Romans came to Britain, they did so not so much in an attempt to trap the druids who flitted back and forth across the English Channel, stirring up revolt and rebellion among the Gaulish tribes on the other side, as to look for wealth. This was in the form of minerals – gold, silver, copper, tin – which had historically provided one of Britain's main trading exports along with the hunting dogs, probably the ancestors of the wolf and deerhounds that we have today all over the Continent. The gold they still mine in small quantities in Wales was used to make Prince Charles's crown when he was invested as Prince of Wales. One of the first things I ever owned was a copper cup in the shape of a goblet, a small chalice, if you like, made from English copper. I never really thought to enquire where it came from until the other day when I was going off to Tattenhall, to the rather good Thai restaurant that lurks incongruously in part of the Bear and Ragged Staff, a fairly robust English pub. And I happened to see a pub named the Copper Mine. On making further enquiries I discovered that the copper mine is still there and that if you take the road up behind the pub you will find it. I also learned that copper is still taken from it, although in fairly small quantities.

There are surely enough of the young generation who want to work with their hands to re-start the mining industries again, although obviously on better terms of employment than in the past, rather than import all our coal and other base minerals from Third World countries where I dread to think what the working conditions are like. In the meantime I think I might just take myself off to the Cheshire copper mine and see if I can lay my hands on some copper and find an artificer to make me another little copper cup.

Broad Bean Pod Purée

June for me is the month for broad beans and my primary broad bean provider, Douglas Wain-Heapy, usually ensures, through my friend Christine, that I'm supplied with some on my birthday. If, like me, you hate having to throw the pods away, here is a suggestion for a good little dish for a summer buffet, which uses up the young broad bean pods.

Broad bean pods

Top and tail the pods and put them into boiling, slightly salted water and cook for about 10 minutes or until a fork goes into them. Strain the broad beans and refresh under cold water. Put your cooked pods through the mouli and you're left with this delicious, intensely broad bean-tasting paste. The thing to do then is to slice some ham thinly, place some broad bean paste in the centre and wrap the ham round it, then lay the wraps out on a dish and serve it on your summer table. Trust me, the flavour is quite, quite delicious.

July

The cuckoo comes in May, he lays his eggs in June,
In July, he must fly

July saw me go to the Althorp Literary Festival. My beloved agent Heather Holden-Brown suggested it, but for some reason, probably tiredness, I thought that it was Aldeburgh, and I had made some sort of vague promise to the booksellers in Aldeburgh to visit so I said yes. I then discovered that I was going somewhere else entirely: Althorp. I was very much in two minds about it because I was never a huge fan of the late Princess Diana and I knew nothing about Charles Spencer other than what I'd seen on television.

Althorp is magnificent, its entrance hall decorated with the most charming scenes of hounds and huntsmen watering their horses. The house is incredibly large, incredibly formal, a bit like the Somerset Maugham Story, 'Alien Corn', in that it's almost too perfect. What it seems to be missing are samplers sewn by maiden aunts hanging among the Rubens, and quirky presents from children propped up on shelves. Charles Spencer, in his interesting book on Althorp and the Spencer family, tells a story of how when he was a small boy, he visited his grandfather with his father and as they were leaving, his father put his hand on to his grandfather's shoulder and squeezed and the old man was overcome and burst into tears. And when they were going Charles Spencer's father explained that the old man was upset because his mother died when he was very small and his wife died in childbirth and he'd had rather a lonely life. The mother who died in childbirth was Charles Spencer's grandmother, which meant that his father in turn had had rather a lonely life and the impression you get in Althorp is that perhaps what it really needs is the consistency of family and people staying there.

I didn't expect to take to Charles Spencer but I found that I liked him enormously. He was intelligent, entertaining and had a real passion for our mutual hero Prince Rupert of the Rhine, who I've always found an intelligent and interesting historic figure, and gave me a copy of his extremely good biography of him. And he endeared himself to me because, having arranged that we should eat out of doors in the portico of the magnificent building that was once the stable block, he determined that we should do so despite the chilly evening. Jackets were therefore supplied for all and sundry. I had actually opened the literary festival by giving my talk before dinner and was so full of adrenalin that I didn't even need a jacket and Charles Spencer and I sat around in our shirt-sleeves while everybody else huddled under rugs and whatever.

It was an excellent dinner. The chef had taken a haunch of muntjac, which is a very suitable size for a dinner party, and had marinated it with oranges and other flavourings and then cooked it on the barbecue and it was quite delicious. To my great pleasure, one of the people involved in the festival who had been a vegetarian for many years and was clearly not in a good way as a result – there are all sorts of ailments you can get if you're a vegetarian for a prolonged period, which stop your amino acid pool and can kill you in the end – said to me, 'Oh, Clarissa, how do I eat meat?' I said, 'Well, why don't you just try a little bit,' and she tried some of the muntjac and really enjoyed it. When I saw her the next day she was delighted that it had had no real adverse affects and I have to say I don't think it was my imagination that she looked much better for it. She said that she would continue to eat meat at least once a month and I rather hope more often than that, but good luck to her.

Of course one of the main sources of protein for the vegetarian is nuts and I think I should tell you about a rather curious phenomenon that came to my attention recently. I have a young friend who has an extremely nice young man with whom she is now co-habiting and he suffers from a severe nut allergy. I have always thought that if you know you're allergic to nuts and likely to go into anaphylactic shock you are therefore extremely careful that you don't eat nuts. What had never occurred to me was the fact that people close to you can't eat them either. My friend has to be extremely careful that she has no contact with nuts of any sort, particularly peanuts, within forty-eight hours of any physical intimacy with her young man. As a result she finds herself, just like people with the allergy, having to ask whether various foods contain nuts or not. While, by law, producers or packagers of products have to state specifically that a product may contain nuts, the same does not necessarily apply to caterers and they may not be quite so careful. So they will no doubt tell you whether there are peanuts or even walnuts in something, but they won't think to tell you that it contains pine kernels or perhaps sesame seeds so that she has to be constantly on her guard as to what she eats. Whether this self-same thing applies to other allergies, I don't at the moment know, but I do think it's something you ought to know about and be very careful.

I am allergic to mushrooms, especially wild mushrooms which I particularly love, which is something that came on a few years ago. I get a very nasty reaction and I know that I've eaten them but it's not in any way potentially fatal. I don't for instance have to carry an anaphylactic shock injection with me in case I unknowingly eat them. I also discovered that these anaphylactic shock injections must not be injected into a vein because you might explode the heart, but have to be injected into muscle. It just shows what you pick up as you go along.

At the dinner I found myself seated next to General Sir Michael Jackson, the former head of the British army, without his Para beret on this occasion. I don't think we liked one another very much and he certainly didn't like me when I said that I lived in Scotland. His response was, 'Oh, well, we don't want to lose Scotland.' And I said that perhaps single-handedly he, with the backing of this present government, had accelerated the chances of the SNP by doing away with the Scottish regiments. When I first came to Scotland, fifteen years ago, if you were on a train that went through the Borders in the late summer and early autumn, there were scores of young men with close-cropped haircuts going off to join the Scottish regiments to build a career and a life for themselves and learn a trade. For some of these young men it was the only family they had. I have, since living in Scotland, seen the benefits of this extended family which of course has now been done away with. If Scotland takes its independence in my lifetime, undoubtedly one of the things that will have brought it about will have been the abolition of the Scottish regiments.

The General had another glass of wine and harrumphed, and I went on to talk to somebody else, who in this instance happened to be Allan Mallinson, whose books I hope you will have read. His hero is a lancer in the period following the Battle of Waterloo, an interesting bit of history that one doesn't know so much about, as one tends to run straight from Waterloo to the Victorians without covering the years in between. He was the most delightful man and I really enjoyed his company and that of his wife. I've seen him since and we've become quite amiable. When I'm asked for my list of people I will invite to my perfect dinner party, he has now joined such names as Charles II and Oscar Wilde and other entertaining figures.

I spent the night in Althorp in a room that was labelled as Princess Diana's dressing room. There were people on the other side of the door in what must have been Princess Diana's bedroom and I said to Allan Mallinson that I felt rather sorry for them because I was prone to snore. He told me the best way to deal with that is to say very loudly, as if I were talking to an old Labrador dog, 'Now lie down and go to sleep on your bed and try not to snore!' which I thought was a very good ruse if not strictly believable.

The Spencers of Althorp have lived there for 500 years. They made their money in sheep in Elizabethan times and it is a house where if at any time the fortunes were supposed to have declined, they didn't decline terribly far. Interestingly, the first Duchess of Marlborough, Sarah Jennings, left her fortune to a relative of hers who was the Spencer of the day. I went to visit the church where generations of Spencers lie under rather cosy little canopies and I felt that poor Diana should have been there with them, rather than out in the middle of the lake on her island. Curiously, during the entire time I was there, no mention was ever made of her.

Another thing that endeared Charles Spencer to me was that he told me he had that very day hosted a group of Americans who had bought lunch and a tour of Althorp at the Countryside

Alliance fundraising auction in America. Altogether, despite my initial misgivings, I was very glad that I had gone to Althorp.

Of course an added bonus of my visit was to convert a vegetarian. It's not that I don't like vegetarians, it's just that I don't understand them. It seems to me that if you don't eat meat because you don't like the way that animals are raised and butchered in this country, if you're lucky enough to buy British meat that is, then the thing to do is to buy meat from those farmers who are rearing livestock properly and producing happy animals who go to meet their maker having had a good life. They taste much better as a result and you are encouraging those particular producers. If I had to eat supermarket meat, I don't think I'd become a vegetarian but the temptation would be there. If you're a vegetarian because you don't like the taste of meat, that's fine. If you're a vegetarian because you love animals and want to convert others to your way of thinking, do you really imagine that people would continue to raise cows and pigs and sheep if there wasn't a market for them? They don't make suitable pets.

A further important point is that being a vegetarian is not a terribly healthy option. Look at the vegetarians you meet who've been that way for a long time and they never appear to be very fit and healthy. Interesting research has been done that shows that among the Dravidian Indian population, who are digestively attuned to a vegetarian diet, the animal protein they get, and of course one doesn't need a huge amount of animal protein, comes from the weevils and the rodent droppings that find their way into the rice and lentils and other pulses. When they come and live in this country, where everything is washed and packaged without such additions, they actually become ill from a lack of animal protein.

July brings the Game Fair which this year was at Blenheim. It moves around, from there to Harewood House and Belvoir Castle as well and it used to go to Romsey but it's no longer held there for whatever reason. It's a curious thing that, however bad the weather for the rest of the summer, the actual period of the Game Fair never fails to be scorching hot. I always take my favourite hat which is from Lock's, the London St James's hatters, and is made of woodchip panama. Its greatest property is that if you dip it into a bucket of water, it holds the water and gradually dries out, thereby keeping your head cool. It doesn't do wonders for your coiffure under it but it does cool your head wonderfully and it's always a great cause of mirth to children who cluster round the stand, watching me dip my hat in the dog bucket and then put it on my head. They wait to see the water cascade over me and of course it doesn't.

I was sitting on the Countryside Alliance stand in the coursing section. The trouble with the Game Fair nowadays is that it has become too big, making it almost impossible to get from A to B even with a disability scooter. I went to do a forum that addressed the antis' new attitudes, in that they'd stopped being balaclava'd thugs and were being more clever in their use of the media. However, it was generally agreed that while they might have set about being more clever they hadn't abandoned being balaclava'd thugs as well. Reports from various hunts around the country showed that they were keeping up their unpleasantries side by side with their new self-imposed role as vigilantes to maintain the law.

When hunting was still legal, the antis would turn up at various events that I was speaking at on my own or together with Johnny Scott, and although they were flagrantly breaking the law, all one's talking to the police could not persuade them to send the antis on their way. I was at a bookshop in Cirencester on one occasion, which had been an old bank and had unbreakable windows. The antis knew this so they stood outside and banged their knees and their fists against the window during this ticketed event and the police, who had been called, simply refused to intervene. When I said that I would go and stand between the antis and the window and see what they did then, the police told me that if I did, they would arrest me for my own good. They do love this attitude of arresting the innocent party for their own good.

Anyway, I did this forum and I didn't know at the time that later on at the Game Fair John Craven and Bill Oddie had a platform in the same ring, or I would have been able to use their presence as an illustration of the changing face of the antis because they are both dyed-in-the-wool supporters of the anti-hunt protestors.

I was however able to make my way to the stand run by Lindsey Knapp, whose Victoria Gallery sells sporting ephemera: pictures and sticks and artefacts generally. I have over the years bought a number of really delightful things from her and I recommend you to her website under the gallery name. This time I was able to have a buy-up and spend some of the money that was burning a hole in my pocket from all my book sales. It's always nice to be at the Game Fair and see all the people that you do see, sometimes from one year to the next. But it's a long hard slog. Although at least I am sitting down, whereas my friends on the coursing stand spend most of their time on their feet talking to people who come to chat to them about the sport.

One of the displays that I always love to go and see at the Game Fair is the poultry pavilion. As I've often said, one of the things I want to do before I die is keep chickens but I'm curious about the fondness that the young seem to have for poultry. The bantams we used to have where I live were readily picked up and carried around by the children when they were younger so that they were regarded as a sort of pet. And a young man of my acquaintance named Harry had a particular affinity with poultry. When at the house that his family have in France, he found a duck egg which he said was abandoned and had no mummy because it was all on its own, so he picked it up. They were just about to come back home to the UK and he brought it with him, carrying it carefully in his hands on the flight over, keeping it warm and cosy. He even succeeded in getting it through all the security. I suppose a duck egg is not going to show up on any scanner and nobody is going to notice a small boy who's standing with his hands in a strange position. Anyway, he brought it back, put it into the incubator that his grandmother had given him, and hatched it! And there was this little French duckling, alive and well, roaming the wilds of the south of England.

Harry is one of those small boys who's noticeably commercially minded, just like my brother who took the shoe cleaning machine back to school with him when he was at Downside and charged everybody sixpence to have their shoes cleaned. Harry moved on to hatching guinea fowl in the incubator which he did with considerable success, selling these birds, mostly by word of mouth, around the country. At first people wanted them to put with their pheasants because they're incredibly good watchdogs. When I was at Danehill on the pheasant shoot, my room overlooked a line of trees where the guinea fowl used to perch at night and, during a full moon, got very little sleep at all because any creature that moved would set them off with that strange, creaking noise they have like a gate that's not working very well.

Guinea fowl eggs are actually very good for baking with because they have quite a large yolk, but you will think that somebody's played a practical joke on you because the shells are so hard to break that it could just as easily be one of those alabaster eggs that you get for cooling your hands on when you're sewing. A good joke to play on people on April Fool's Day is to give them a boiled guinea fowl egg for breakfast and watch them try to get into it. I always find it very strange to see these dumpy little birds from the African veldt clacking around the English countryside. But I suppose it's quite appropriate when I'm told that most fishing flies nowadays that people use to fish on our local rivers are made in Kenya where the women's deft little fingers are perfect for the work. I'm happier to think of them making fishing flies than picking and packing asparagus for Marks and Spencer. They might earn money from the fishing flies and be able to eat the asparagus themselves, or at least grow something for their own consumption.

Young Harry built up a thriving trade with his guinea fowl and his grandmother said to me, 'For heaven's sake don't tell him that people might be eating them!' So I didn't say anything to him, until one day some time later I asked, 'Harry, what do you think people do with your guinea fowl once they've acquired them from you?' And he said, 'Oh, I don't know, Clarissa – I expect they probably eat them.'

Flush with his success from the guinea fowl, Harry has now moved on to the Italian quail which really takes me back to my childhood; when I was young and visiting in Sussex, the largest quail farm in the country was in some barns just below

Bo Peep, the big chalk quarry on the road up to Firle Beacon, and if you went past in summer the smell was quite appalling. I don't think they were being kept in particularly bad conditions, it was just that guano from most poultry doesn't smell very nice and particularly not from quails.

I have never shot, nor indeed been to watch wild quail shooting in America but I gather that they provide very good sport because they are very small, quick and deft, but I do like to eat quail. I think it is a bird that is singularly underrated in this country, and with which you can do a lot of interesting things. In my *Game Cookbook* which I wrote with Johnny Scott we give a Greek recipe for quail cooked in clay that is quite fun. You put a lot of spices inside the quail, then you oil the outside and wrap it in clay and cook it; you bring it to the table still in its little clay wrapper which you then break open to reveal the cooked quail all ready to eat.

Apparently if you give a quail a drop of whisky it becomes very belligerent and fights with other quails like mad, and I understand that if you go to an Indian restaurant and find that the special on that day is quail, you're actually eating the evidence of the quail fight that took place in the Pakistani community the night before. As with cock fighting, I've never been to a quail fight, but I gather that it is very popular in South-East Asia as well. It has always been a mystery to me why parliamentarians think that if you ban something it will automatically stop. You only have to look at soccer. After all, there are still two bills on the statute book banning soccer, one from the reign of Henry VIII and one from the reign of James II and look how successful they've been.

Young Harry's quail live in a rather splendid two-tier edifice because quail like to have an upstairs and a downstairs in their lives. He and his siblings also hatch the rather more rarefied bantams that his mother loves dearly, and I do think what a good thing it is for children who are interested in animal husbandry to have an incubator. It's a constant source of entertainment watching the young birds hatching and having the chicks around the place, which are also a potential source of profit, selling them on and perhaps going to poultry sales. Be warned that you have to be careful nowadays if you have the rarer sorts of bantams and hens because people nick them. I know somebody who had some bantams in a pen in a paddock and some passing vagabonds came over the fence and nicked the lot and presumably sold them off in the local poultry sale.

Apart from providing fresh eggs, what a friend of mine calls 'from bum to consumer', the birds also, when they come to the end of their days, provide a boiling fowl. I know that people become very sentimental about their poultry, especially if you're keeping them in an Eglu in the garden, but I think that when you have to knock them on the head you might as well eat them; there is nothing quite as good as an old boiling fowl, cooked very slowly and gently either in small beer or cider, and perhaps stuffed with fruit in the manner of the Derbyshire speciality, Hindle Wakes. If you cook it properly you'll have a large bird that is infinitely tender and delicious. When I was living in Sussex in the late seventies, if you went to Lewes market at the right time of the year you would find young cockerels that had been knocked on the head, because of course you can't have more than one cockerel in a farmyard or all you'll get is cockfights, and were being sold at a very reasonable price at a weight of about nine or ten pounds. You would take these home and cook them, obviously rather slowly because a cockerel is quite a muscular animal and the flavour was superb. As Jennifer used to say, 'There's an awful lot of good in an old cock.' And the same applies to a young one too.

It's almost impossible to buy a boiling fowl nowadays. Sometimes you can get them in the Chinese supermarkets, where they're sold under the title 'old hen'. I know one woman, for instance, who raises chickens for eggs on the Woldingham Estate and I once said to her, 'Could I perhaps, when you come to knock them on the head, bag a boiling fowl?' and she said, 'Oh no, we don't do that – we let them die happily.' That is a form of sentimentality that is quite beyond me. People say to me, how would you like to be eaten when you die? And actually I wouldn't mind at all, except that cannibalism is illegal. After all the incredibly delicious and expensive things I've eaten throughout my life, I might make quite an interesting meal. When I was young, one of the features of meals with people who had chickens would be a boiling fowl and I can remember cleaning them and finding a number of unformed eggs in the egg duct and being told to separate them out and put them aside to stuff the chicken with because they were delicious and had a very good flavour. We also used to serve poached chicken with rice and a white sauce. Nowadays if you go around the farmers' markets and see people selling off boiling fowl, they're just rather mature chickens.

The difference in both taste and appearance between a genuinely free-range hen's egg and an ordinary hen's egg is quite amazing. When I was young we'd stop at a farm near Chalvington to buy eggs. There were always chickens wandering around pecking at the ground and I don't know what breed of hen they were or indeed what they ate but the eggs were practically square and you could see the squeeze marks on the shell. Obviously the hens had eaten a lot of grit as well but they were wonderful eggs.

Once, filming for *Two Fat Ladies* at Kylemoor Abbey in Ireland, the eggs served in the hotel where we were staying were laid by their own chickens and had yolks that were almost tangerine. Over my breakfast boiled egg I said to the woman, 'Good Lord, what are you feeding your hens on?' 'Sure,' she said, 'isn't it something they find in the woods.' But the flavour was quite unique and delicious.

My great-aunt Jess had been born on a sailing ship, which always used to fascinate me. Not only had an officer on the sailing ship painted a picture of the ship for her to grow up with but also her birth certificate, which was registered at the port of London, gave the latitude and longitude of her birthplace. When we looked it up for her, she was born coming through Hell's Gates just outside Avon. I expect her mother probably agreed with the latitude and longitude. Jess and her husband Bertie kept chickens and they were the first ones I had ever really come across, although Uncle Bertie used to call them his hens.

On one occasion I went into the kitchen and there on the Aga was a saucepan bubbling away and I asked what was in it. Auntie Jess lifted the lid to reveal a sort of boiling mulch of potato peelings and other bits and pieces for chicken food because in those days you took all your leftovers and you fed them to the chickens, which will eat anything. Rather like pigs, they are excellent food converters and you will get a very good return on your rubbish. The local councils who set up all these ecological bins would perhaps be well minded to tell people to feed their food waste to chickens. Up until and during the Second World War I gather there used to be swill bins on every corner and people would take their food waste to the swill bins which would then be collected by the council and fed to the pigs. You can't do that now, because you have to have licences for feeding swill, which has to be boiled to a particular temperature before you can feed it to the pigs, but it seems to me it would be an excellent way of coping with the problem of food waste and again converting it into food.

Young Harry is now growing into a fine, handsome young man and is a very good cricketer and rugby player, but I hope he doesn't give up his interest in poultry. In Victorian times, raising not only the more rarefied types of chicken but also all sorts of different pigeons was very popular and the Victorians bred, not just racing pigeons but all the tumblers and display pigeons that you see with their extraordinary fan tails. Johnny Scott told me that he was once travelling through the Borders and came upon a sort of hallucinogenic show of different coloured pigeons twirling about in the dying sun. Convinced that it couldn't just be the natural light of the sun, he went to investigate and discovered that the chap who bred them dyed them with assorted vegetable dyes just for the sheer pleasure of watching the display they made.

I cannot understand why we import an enormous quantity of squab pigeons each year from Italy, France and America, when the countryside is full of empty pigeon lofts in which we could restore the living larder that was so popular in previous times, and provide our own delicious dinner of pigeon.

Thinking of different extraordinary-looking breeds, I'm reminded of that charming short story by Saki, H.H. Munro, of a man who was so bored travelling up and down to London on the train that he started making up stories and the more far-fetched the story, the more his fellow passengers believed it. Until, that is, he told them one day about a snake that got into a hen run and killed all the hens, except for this one rare type of hen that was probably an Araucana which had a fringe right down over its eyes so that the snake couldn't mesmerise it, and it killed the snake. This was actually a true story which he was agog to tell his friends but they wouldn't believe him and they ostracised him and he had to go and sit in a different compartment thereafter.

Even if you're not a poultry aficionado, next time you're at a game fair or a country fair, take yourself to the poultry tent, because you will see the most amazing variety of breeds and some of them are really quite beautiful. Somebody I knew once bred a partridge wine dot chicken which was rather like a game fowl, but had the most beautiful colouring on its feathers. And I do think that the chicken is one of the more unappreciated birds. There is nothing like hens clucking around and the strange sort of almost purring noises they sometimes make to give one a sense of wellbeing and peace. As long as you can keep them away from the foxes and the badgers, who will have them before you will, they are a joy and a delight.

One of the creatures I don't want to keep again in my life are geese. That seems a little unfair to geese, but they are noisy (being also very good watchmen), quite messy and fierce. When I was a child, my friend Christine's family used to have a goose called Forty Watts because he'd been hatched under a forty-watt bulb, and he used to come up on to the lawn at teatime and eat cucumber sandwiches and be generally very agreeable. But they also had a flock of geese in the spinney and when we went to play in the tree-house we used to have to run away from them because they would come and peck the backs of our legs quite nastily and generally be really fierce and frightening.

Geese, for those of you who do keep them, will not interbreed into the first degree of cousinry, if not the second, so that very often you can think you've got a barren gander when in fact all you've got is one that's too closely related to the females. I remember discovering this when I was working at Danehill and a friend of mine, June Coleman, had the same problem so we agreed to swap our ganders. I put my gander in a sack in the back of the car and set off across country and stopped in Uckfield to go to the baker. I should point out that this was during my drinking days when my brain was perhaps not as sharp as it might have been. I went into the Indian restaurant, had a quick something to eat and then returned to the car. By this time I'd completely forgotten about the goose which was still in his sack in the back of the car and I suddenly heard this unearthly noise and looking in my rear-view mirror I saw this white shape swaying backward and forward and making a very strange noise and I thought, Dear God it's finally happened, I've got the DTs at last. But then I remembered that it was the gander and went on to my destination. We duly swapped our ganders and I brought the other one back without any mishaps and there were lots of little goslings a bit later on that year.

Geese are incredibly difficult to kill. The best way is to use a broomstick and put it on either side of the neck and stand on the broomstick and pull its head back. They're also incredibly difficult to pluck, very tough on the fingers, but they make very good eating and of course goose fat is a delicious cooking agent.

I might as well round up with turkeys which I seem not to have mentioned. Don't keep them. They're neurotic, difficult and although a properly raised turkey tastes considerably better than anything you'll buy, except perhaps from Tom Copas, it does mean that you will not get a lot of pleasure from it. Turkeys are simply not good pets.

And all this rifling from little Harry's duck egg – just think about it!

Raspberry soufflé omelette

This is something we used to have at home, though I've never had it anywhere else. I believe it is a Viennese dish but I have only my mother's word for this.

a large punnet of raspberries
some castor sugar
4 good size eggs
some butter

Take about a tablespoon of raspberries aside and put them in a bowl and sprinkle them with castor sugar and leave them in a warm place to bleed. You'll then put them through a sieve in order to get some juice. Separate your eggs and stiffly beat the whites. Then fold in the lightly whisked egg yolks. Heat your omelette pan and melt the butter. Pour the omelette mixture into the pan and it will rise. When it is almost cooked, put in the unsugared raspberries and let it cook a little longer and fold the omelette over. Then take your strained juice and just as you are about to serve, pour it over the top and sprinkle on a little icing sugar.

August

Red sky at night, shepherd's delight
Red sky in the morning, shepherd's warning

August came and the Glorious Twelfth brought in the grouse shooting season. There were not that many grouse this year. Grouse numbers come and go, and because grouse are a wild bird you can't bring them into captivity. They're badly affected by cold or wet springs and even by the state of the heather and whether the heather moorland is properly kept, although now that grouse shooting is so expensive I think much more attention is paid to the heather.

People assume that the heather moorlands grow of their own accord, but this is not the case. The heather moorlands were developed by the shepherds in the 1890s as grazing for their sheep and they dug drains to keep the wet away from the heather roots, thereby killing off the heather beetle which is now making a comeback. If you see a heather hill that is a rusty colour rather than purple that's because it is being attacked by the heather beetle. If grouse shooting were to be banned, as the antis would have it, and people were not interested in maintaining the heather moorland, it would return to white scrub as it was before this period. If you want to learn more about the management of heather moorland, I would recommend you to the Heather Trust website whose vice-president is Johnny Scott.

This year brings back memories of my last outing on a grouse shoot, which was at Drumlanrig, the Dumfriesshire home of my dear late friend, Johnnie, Duke of Buccleuch. The Buccleuch family are one of the largest private landowners in Britain, with three estates in Scotland and one in England and have a tradition of enlightened stewardship of their estates. They also have royal links, being descended from the Duke of Monmouth, the eldest 'allegedly' illegitimate son of Charles II. It was the last year of Johnnie's life when I went to stay. He's a man who I respected more than anybody, probably, I've ever known. He was a force for good, outspoken, sensible, always able to put up a good argument rather than just a rant, and all this from his wheelchair in which he spent nearly the last forty years of his life, as a result of a hunting accident. Staying in a castle like Drumlanrig, which is a beautiful Renaissance edifice constructed of pink sandstone, is always an exciting experience. My bedroom was so large that one could have had a very good party in it without actually noticing that it was taking place. I'd been to Drumlanrig before, for the rather disappointing launch of the Buccleuch Heritage Foods, and it is truly magnificent. The estate itself is very extensive, amounting to some 120,000 acres, over which they shot grouse on two days. It was a real pleasure to see James Percy, who is accounted one of the best shots in the country, at work, and also to see dear Max Hastings, the author and journalist, who is a very keen and clever shot, but is also a great source of entertainment at dinner.

On one of the days I was driven round by Johnnie himself in his Volvo estate which he drove with such dash and élan that it would have been all too easy to forget that he'd lost the use of his legs. We went over roads that he would have known as a boy and bounced about in the car with great enthusiasm. While I was there he took me to see the Museum of Lead Mining at Wanlockhead because he said they had a very good café. And indeed he was right. One forgets that these hills were a great source of lead and other minerals which helped to found the Buccleuch family fortunes. On the third day they shot partridges which were flighted across the valley from one hill to the next with the guns below, so, if you like, they were artificially high birds. I was quite glad that I had decided not to take my gun on my visit because what with the speed of the grouse and the height of the partridges I think I might have had an embarrassing sojourn.

It was the last time I was to see Johnnie, and sadly I was unable to get to his funeral nor to either of his memorial services due to the frenzy of my bookings, but I shall always carry his memory in my mind and my heart. I therefore didn't really need to attend the services, but I would have liked to have done so as a mark of respect.

I remember the first time I met him was at Bowhill, his home in the Borders, when he was launching his Buccleuch beef initiative which I had accidentally become involved in through my friend Colin Taylor, the man who was responsible for my becoming a member of the Worshipful Company of Butchers. My favourite story that day was about a rather chippy member of the council who came up from Selkirk when the regulations for keeping grand houses open to the public in line with the Disability Acts were introduced. Obviously nobody had told him about Johnnie because he arrived, full of himself and how he was going to tell them how to proceed, and was rather deflated to be greeted at the door by Johnnie himself, in his wheelchair, who said, 'Oh, have you come to see what we've done here? I think I can say that I've had a great deal of experience and will be able to assist you.' As we gathered in the hall at Bowhill, my attention was taken by a large picture of a little boy with red-gold curls, wearing a kilt and playing with a Border terrier. I said to Johnny, 'What an enchanting little boy. One would really like to become friends with him.' He said, 'Well, I hope you are now doing so.' And he added, 'I had hair in those days.' I shall certainly miss him.

Incidentally, this is not a recommendation to you to buy Buccleuch beef, as these days it is not what is was when Johnnie started the project. Most of the farmers who were supplying the beef, which became so famous and sought after in every London restaurant, now deal with Rory Duff of MacDuff.

It was Max Hastings who was responsible for Michel Roux and I inventing carpaccio of grouse. We were staying at Conholt when he said, 'I love grouse, I love it so rare that I could really eat it raw.' And Michel and I looked at one another and said, 'Carpaccio!' And so if you look in my *Game Cookbook*, you will find the recipe. What is particularly good about this dish is that it is an excellent way of using an older bird, which doesn't respond to roasting so well as a younger one. I love grouse and I have to say that in my various sojourns at the Goring Hotel in London this summer, I was able to eat it quite often; they do it terribly well and cook it beautifully.

There's a lovely story that came out of Yorkshire where the antis went to disrupt a shoot on a grouse moor. Some time during the course of the day, the mist came down quite thickly and the guns and beaters packed up and went home. The antis had followed the shoot up and now found that they were lost on the moor, so by dint of having a mobile phone they rang the police. The police, who knew perfectly well who they were and what was going on, when told that the antis needed rescuing, said quite rightly that it wasn't very cold, the weather was relatively mild and the mist might lift – if not straight away it would certainly lift in the morning – so suggested that they should ring again in the morning if they were still lost. The antis therefore spent a cold and uncomfortable night on the moor and eventually made their way down in the morning. It seems to me the correct way to deal with them. Don't think that these are nice, fluffy, sweet people. A group of them stopped a keeper's wife up here on the Lammermuirs while she was driving home and told her that if she didn't stop her husband being a keeper, she would have acid thrown in her face. The poor woman was totally traumatised and verging on a breakdown as a result.

Let me tell you a bit about *Lagopus lagopus*, the red grouse, because in talking to my urban friends I've realised that people don't really know about these things. The red grouse is one of a group of the grouse family found in the United Kingdom. At the top of the tree is the biggest, the capercaillie, a huge bird the size of a turkey which lives in the pine forests in the north of Scotland. Sadly there are not too many of them left in the area because the RSPB acquired the Abernethy Estate, which has most of the native pines, and as that organisation has a policy of not killing raptors, the capercaillie population has been reduced to a very few breeding pairs. They're now more widely found in the pine forests of Scandinavia. Capercaillie are very shy birds that hide away. If you do try to eat them, they taste very heavily of resin, rather like that disgusting wine, retsina, that you get in Greece. There are also the black grouse, or black game, which although not good to eat are delightful to watch during the mating season when they perform a complicated and rather exotic dance known as the lek. And finally the ptarmigan; it was Edward VII who said that he'd never go to a house again that served ptarmigan. I should think, given the habits of Edward VII, that people were probably queuing up to feed him ptarmigan. Again, it's not a terribly delicious bird. The best of them all is without doubt the red grouse.

It's quite difficult to keep grouse on a grouse moor. They're ground-nesting birds with all that implies, so a wet, cold spring means that not only are the chicks in danger of drowning or dying of cold, but also that there isn't the insect life for them to feed on in their first few weeks of life before they turn vegetarian and eat heather shoots. If the heather is not properly kept, and not burned back regularly the shoots will be too high for the chicks to eat and so they'll starve. Grouse are also prone to tick infestation which is one of the reasons for keeping sheep on a grouse moor. The sheep go bungling through the heather and the ticks attach themselves to the sheep because they're a large, warm animal, much easier to find than the little grouse. The sheep are then dipped and that kills the ticks on their wool and therefore reduces the tick population.

Another problem is vermin, animals such as foxes, stoats and weasels, which will not only kill the chicks but will eat the eggs too. Raptors pose a threat as well, because grouse are very prone to attack from birds of prey. The Duke of Buccleuch lent his Langholm grouse moor to the RSPB to prove his point that raptors, if left unchecked, take grouse to the point of extinction. The subsequent increase in peregrine falcons was so great that within ten years there was not a single grouse left on the moor. And grouse don't come back, so a perfectly good moor was ruined because of sentiment about hawks. The whole RSPB love affair with raptors is a complete mystery to me. Maybe it's because they're more dramatic to look at than, say, a songbird and that brings in the tourists, who bring in the bucks to the RSPB reserves. That might sound a little unkind but, you know, if you don't maintain a balance in nature there ain't gonna be

no nature, as they discovered on Zanzibar when they ⸝
in a whole lot of crows to eat the rubbish on the rubbish tips
and all the crows did was eat the local songbirds so that there are
now only crows on Zanzibar.

The Flint and Danby moors in North Wales were said to
be the best grouse moors in Europe and much sought after as
a shooting venue. But the forestry that was heavily planted in
recent years by the Forestry Commission provided a home for
vermin. Little Grey Rabbit was right, you know: bad things
live in the deep dark wood and now there is not a single red
grouse left on the grouse moors and very few black game at
that. Shooting grouse is not easy. They fly just over the tops of
the heather at eighty miles an hour straight towards you. Very
often the weather is dark, as is the skyline, and so you have
little chance to see them before they're upon you. There is a
wonderful book called *The Glorious Twelfth* written by my nun
friend April O'Leary's godfather, where an army colonel who
is a mad keen grouse shot falls into a coma and finds himself as
a grouse on the Glorious Twelfth. It's a delightful story, and no
longer in print but you can find it in second-hand shops.

Nowadays if you celebrate the Glorious Twelfth by eating
grouse in a London restaurant I should warn you that it is very
probably last year's grouse, frozen and preserved for precisely
that date.

Curiously, as I was writing this, I received a text message
from a young man called Wiggy, son of friends of mine, who
is currently studying at Ballymaloe Cookery School and you
would have been mystified by the message because it said, 'I'll
provide the falcon if you provide the hat.'

This came about because at a dinner party a keen falconer
was flirting with my friend and, presumably imagining this was

Anyway, what did I do on returning home? The Olympics were on, and for the first time in my life I acquired a television set, something I've always avoided doing but I was so exhausted and so tired that all I wanted to do was sit and slump and so I watched the Olympics. Our splendid successes in the medal tables, I was happy to notice, were given their proper credit; that is to former Prime Minister John Major, himself a fine athlete and cricketer, who encouraged the promotion of sport through lottery funding and clearly it paid off. I must remember when 2012 comes to make quite certain that I not only have a television set but that I don't go anywhere near London.

When I was staying at the Goring Hotel I met a woman whom Ken Livingstone had brought over to advise on the Cross London Rail Link which will run to the East End for the Olympics and she told me, back then before the election of Boris Johnson as London mayor, that the Cross Rail Link would not be in place until 2020. So quite how people are going to get to the East End for the Olympics seems something of a mystery.

The other show I went to see in the Festival was a production of T.S. Eliot's *Murder in the Cathedral*. We went because Trevor Harding, my heroic septuagenarian roofing expert, was playing one of the Knights. And curiously Richard Holloway, erstwhile Bishop of Edinburgh, was playing Thomas Becket. It was an interesting piece of casting, but interesting is all I think it amounted to. One forgets quite how tedious Eliot can be. Great to read some of his poetry but as a playwright, he lacked an editor.

The rest of the time I stayed home.

My father was something of a pyromaniac; he loved having fires in the house, bonfires outside the house and I used to be very caustic about this when I was young. Especially as at the slightest touch of cool weather in the middle of summer he would light a fire. There was quite a lot of cool weather this August in the evening and surprisingly I found myself lighting fires. What's that verse you see on cushions, 'Mirror, mirror on the wall, I am my mother after all' – or in this particular case, my father. Possibly because of that, and watching those enthusiastic young competing for their medals, I was reminded of the days when I was quite a good athlete, or quite a good swimmer anyway, and was regarded as an Olympic potential and that got me to thinking about life and death.

I've lost a number of friends over the last few years and perhaps my fading eyesight was the catalyst for me to indulge in a rare instance of feeling sorry for myself. However, death is not something I fear. I suppose all my years as an alcoholic made it too good a friend. I can remember sitting there opening the next bottle of gin and wondering if this would be the one that killed me. I had said when I started drinking, in my last conversation with the Almighty until the end of my drinking days, 'Okay, God, let's play Russian roulette.' And many years down the line, the Catholic priest who took me to my first AA meeting and who is also in recovery, said to me, 'Whatever made you think that God would load the revolver? You can't make terms like that with God.' But at that time had I believed that there was nothing out there and death was just a hole in the ground, who knows what might have happened? The combination of my Catholic upbringing and belief in something in the hereafter, although I don't really see myself sitting on a cloud playing a dulcimer or eating manna (I don't have much of a sweet tooth), stopped me.

What do I believe? More and more as I get older, I believe in reincarnation – don't laugh. Something like two-thirds of the world believes in reincarnation, it's only the Judaeo-Islamic-Christian belt that doesn't. When I was at school, aged about thirteen or fourteen, I read a book by Alfred Noyes, which consisted of three stories that were supposed to illustrate reincarnation; there was a poem at the front of the book which I don't really remember, except that it said why should a god who sees every bird that falls, squander souls? It's always seemed to me that if there is a point in life, and I believe there is, then it is about dealing with and solving and facing up to specific problems, just like a hand of cards that you have been dealt this time around. Then you're ready to move on to the next set of problems. There is no way in this life that you can deal with every question that could possibly be raised. I also once read somewhere that if you felt particularly strongly about something, either for or against it, and you had no particular reason to do so, then maybe it was connected with your past and you had been there before.

If I walk into a mid-eighteenth-century kitchen as I did at Sulgrave Manor when I was making the Hannah Glasse programme, I roll up my sleeves. All the flavours I love are those of that particular period, anchovies and capers and so forth. I remember when I first moved to Scotland and was feeling quite miserable because I'd been sacked from Books for Cooks, which had been my focus for the first seven years of my recovery, turning that shop into a household name, I used to like to go and sit in the kitchens of the Georgian House in Charlotte Square. These are state-of-the-art Georgian kitchens, even to the extent of having the first spit that turned faster or slower depending on the amount of smoke going up the chimney, so that if you put on more wood it burned hotter and the spit would turn faster.

My comfort food is Chinese, and the one set of foreigners that I am really drawn to are the Chinese. People often say that I have Chinese hands and feet. In my case, my feet are now so bad that if I was Chinese in a previous life, they were probably bound. This is all whimsy but it's curious where your mind can take you. Anyway, please don't send me sackfuls of letters telling me that I'm mad, or explaining your views on reincarnation or heaven because everybody's beliefs are personal to them.

I mentioned Lord Elphinstone earlier on and I live very close to an estate called Carberry, which used to be the Elphinstone estate. It was gifted to the Church of Scotland in the late 1960s and is now run as a venue for conferences, parties and the like, as well as having rooms to stay in. That's where we held my landlord Harry's eightieth birthday party. It was his wife, Marianne, who came up with the title for *Spilling the Beans*, which I thought terribly clever. I think she's come up trumps again with her suggestion of *Rifling Through My Drawers* which I find very funny, but I dare say the publishers will come up with something deeply pedestrian. We'll see. Anyway, Marianne suggested to the chefs at Carberry that they should cook recipes out of various of my cookery books, which was a good way of escaping from the usual rather boring, mass-catering menus of farmed salmon or over-cooked beef, or, worst of all and heavens do I know this one, rubber chicken. They produced a good cross-section of my recipes which I have to say the chefs did extremely well.

The last Elphinstones to live at Carberry were the 16th Earl and Countess. She was the Queen Mother's sister. Unfortunately she had rather a penchant for the drink and when it took her, off she would go down to the Commercial Hotel in Musselburgh and dance on the tables. The citizens of Musselburgh found this upsetting and complained to the Earl, who remonstrated with his wife; she accepted that this was quite embarrassing for the local people so she transferred her libidinous activities to Leith. In those days Leith was still a working port and was pretty rough and she would go and dance on the tables and entertain the sailors, which gave rise to an expression in Musselburgh of somebody who was behaving badly which was: 'Just like old Lady Elphinstone'. I first came across this when the dog from the main house – a rescue lurcher from Craigmillar, one of the rougher areas of Edinburgh, if not the roughest – came into season, disappeared for three days and came back looking rather battered and Mrs Davidson, the housekeeper in the big house, said, 'Och, just like old Lady Elphinstone.'

It was strange to be home after so long. In the previous thirteen months I had been home for a total of only thirteen weeks. The house had been transformed and I would like to pause here and pay tribute to Amelia. She describes herself as my housekeeper (personally I don't think six hours a week makes a housekeeper) but I would describe her as my friend. She looks after me terribly well, both when I'm here and in my absence when she says it gets rather boring because she's reduced to cleaning the rather nice Scottish School art nouveau fireplace which is made of copper and comes up a treat when it's polished. Amelia has been with me now for fourteen years and it must drive her nuts because if I'm working, which I am when I'm home, then I have piles of books and papers which she's not allowed to put away or move, but has to dust around. On occasion she has come and helped me with cookery demonstrations and done very well. I'm happy to say that for a birthday present some years ago I gave her and her husband a trip to Dublin for a long weekend. At that point she'd never been out of Scotland before and now she's a world traveller, going much further afield than I do and to all sorts of interesting places like Bosnia and Portugal. Amelia has a great sense of humour and says that when she wins the lottery she'll buy a house in the village so that she can invite me for coffee because we always have a good cup of coffee before she starts her work.

I'm very particular about my coffee. I only like cafetiere coffee and I really only like Java or Sumatra freshly ground. Curiously the Arabic name for coffee is the same as the Arabic word for alcohol and I'm sure that while I don't consume the amount of coffee that I did of gin, I've become equally addicted, but only to good coffee. I buy my coffee beans from a delicatessen in Edinburgh on Dundas Street called Glass and Thompson, where they serve what is undoubtedly the best coffee in Edinburgh and is run by a somewhat eccentric New Zealander called Russell. They also have a tempting array of baked goods.

Mercifully, my addiction to coffee doesn't have the shattering effects of alcohol, despite what doctors may tell you. I'm not a great believer in the National Health Service. The one and only time I ever had an operation on the NHS was on my umbilical hernia and as far as I could see, they tried to kill me. It was so badly done that the Spanish surgeon who had to repair the damage as an emergency told me that the stitches were far too small, far too close together and some of them were sewn into necrotic tissue. The end result was that the whole thing pulled out and nearly led to my demise.

When I was in the recovery centre, Promis, I had no money, having spent it all, and I couldn't have got an assisted bed because the regulations say you have to be clean for at least four weeks before you go into treatment but don't really suggest how you're going to get clean if you were as chronic an alcoholic as

I was. And so consequently the NHS wouldn't pay for me. In any event, they only pay for very few assisted beds in treatment centres a year.

I'm fascinated by the attitude of the medical profession to alcoholism. Although the World Health Authority recognises it as an illness, the British medical profession won't do so. Presumably this is under pressure from the insurance industry, because if it's an illness you can get treated for it on your health insurance and therefore also, theoretically at least, on the NHS. But the general attitude is that you should pull up your socks. Although when I was in Amberstone, which was the detox centre for Hellingly Hospital in East Sussex, in my first unsuccessful attempt to stop drinking, their attitude was that alcoholics simply didn't get better. Most of the medics I come across – and don't forget that I'm related to an awful lot of medics because my father was one of nine children and all the boys went into one form of medicine or another and all the girls married into the medical profession, apart from my Auntie Holly and then her son became professor of anatomy – think of it as simply an untreatable condition best dealt with by some Valium and self-discipline. And yet, before their very eyes is evidence of so many people who have successfully got well and lead good, active and productive lives and support themselves through the twelve-step fellowships. But if you go to the doctor seeking help, in most cases they'll look no further than to put you on pills.

If you go round, as a lot of us do, asking the various surgeries if we can put up notices about the number to ring for Alcoholics Anonymous, they're not really interested and even if they agree, you put it up, but the next time you go round, it isn't there any more. The only conclusion that I could come to was that the medical profession do not approve of the twelve-step fellowships because they are not in control of the situation. Like Aristotle I'm a cynic: if there ain't no money in it, there ain't no power in it and there ain't no glory in it if you tell somebody to go off to Alcoholics Anonymous and put their small donation in the pot. Because where is the benefit to the medical profession?

I have seen too many of my friends die because general practitioners are allowed something like only five or six minutes to see a patient and by the time they get round to recognising that the pain in the back or the cough in the throat or so many other symptoms are in fact something more serious, in both these instances cancer, it's too late. Again I wonder cynically if late diagnosis in people over a certain age isn't the cheaper, softer option. What a terrible suggestion for a profession that won't allow people to die when they want to, or when their lives are clearly over, because I suppose they get money for the geriatric beds too and they can experiment on the Alzheimer cases. I know that when my time comes, if I have to, I'll be off to Switzerland like a shot. Although as my friend Christine said to me, 'Don't think that I'm going to take you to Dignitas.' And I said, 'My dear, they'll be queuing up to take me!' But hopefully I'm a long way from that and I really must start cultivating the poison garden. I did once have a climbing aconite plant. Because it died back in winter, my window of time in which I could have chewed it and topped myself was rather small and as my friend Maggy said, 'Well, if you lose your marbles and we find you chewing on the clematis, we'll point you in the right direction.'

In an era where belief in God and the hereafter has become unfashionable and greed and Mammon are all the rage, people do seem to want to stay alive beyond their sell-by date. I suppose the one exception to that is the Muslim martyrs, as they would call themselves, who can't wait to get over there to their seventy-five virgins. The Koran states very specifically that women are hollow vessels and we don't have souls so I've never really found myself particularly drawn towards Islam. I gather that if you see an Arab family walking across a minefield, the wife goes first, then the donkey and then the husband.

I don't understand why the feminist groups and the women's rights groups have not got themselves involved in the whole question of arranged marriages, of so-called honour killings, of forced burnings or the various abuses that women suffer at the hands of fundamentalist Islam. However on the converse side, one is reminded of that amazing female, Afghan warlord Bibi Ayesha, known as 'the Pigeon', who goes into battle always accompanied by a male member of her family so that she's not breaking the tenets of the Koran, dressed in her burka, face veiled but with her ammunition belt strapped across her when she goes in to fight. She is even, I believe, the proud possessor of a captured tank. But if she can get away with it, then why are other Islamic women not standing up to be counted? Anyway, enough of this before I get a fatwa.

So after three weeks I dragged myself away from my dear little house and went south again. I went away to umpire a cricket match. I love cricket. I grew up in the shadow of Lord's Cricket Ground and my girlhood heroes were cricketers, not pop stars: the Bedser twins, Fred Titmus, Ken Barrington, Colin Cowdray. I sound like that charming poem: ' . . . as the run stealers flicker to and fro, to and fro, O my Hornby and my Barlow long ago!' These are names that perhaps mean nothing to any of you. For me the only good way to spend a summer afternoon is by a cricket pitch or, better still, on a cricket pitch, umpiring. I played cricket at school, where I was captain of cricket, but it was not something that I had any wish to carry on beyond schooldays and I then found that scoring was not enough. Sitting by the side of the boundary left me frustrated and so I learned the skills of umpiring and became an accredited umpire at village competition level. I don't do it so much nowadays. I suspect the batsmen object that they can't see round me to the bowler.

This particular match was an inter-hunt match between the Southern Shires Bloodhounds, the New Forest Hounds and the New Forest Beagles. It started as a three-handed match and I was asked to umpire it a few years ago and then they decided that it would include a fourth team, the coursing team. To date it has been organised by the Bloodhounds under the auspices of their master, Mark Winchester, who takes the whole thing terribly seriously and provides a very efficient team as well as a delicious lunch.

I have a slight problem with bloodhounds. They were originally bred for chasing fugitives, for running down runaway slaves and escaped prisoners and perhaps in my subconscious I identify with the quarry. But also I do prefer, or at least have done, to follow hunts that actually kill their quarry. Then I had a divine idea and I said to Mark, 'If only your bloodhounds could be trained to run down Labour politicians, preferably Labour cabinet ministers, I'd feel much more kindly disposed towards them,' and he said he'd see what he could do. The hounds follow the scent of a runner who sets off across country and there's a charming description in *Love in a Cold Climate* of the children being the quarry and excitedly setting off to lay the scent and how horrified the neighbours are because these children are being pursued by these huge dogs. Bloodhounds are in fact very big, they're the largest of the hound family, and with their lugubrious faces, long ears and black and tan colouring, can look quite frightening. They have this deep, deep bay which I should think would put fear into any fugitive.

The match is played at a cricket ground in Hampshire and as always in this type of match, there's a lot of last-minute cancellations and ringing up your friends to see if they're free to play and one has a very jolly time. In the first couple of years Bloodhounds triumphed quite easily because they had far and away the best players. But in later years the other hunts have pulled up their socks and the coursing team, I have to say, acquitted itself quite splendidly although failed to win.

As I said, I was the umpire and very much enjoyed it. Cricket (and this is why I enjoy being out by the wicket) is a game of chess. The positioning of the fielders represents the positioning of the chessmen on a chessboard. To me it's more exciting than a game of chess because not only do you have the players' actions but also the state of the wicket plays a part, and is influenced by the weather as much as by the groundsmen. When I used to umpire down in Sussex there were certain grounds that were under the loom of the Downs, where the cloud cover and the barometric pressure had an enormous influence on what the ball did. In those sorts of conditions you could see a slow bowler or a spin bowler move the ball with amazing dexterity and because of the barometric pressure you'd get six balls in an over that all moved in a totally different manner, something you don't see quite so clearly from the boundary. Curiously, despite all the technology involved in televising cricket, you don't really get the feel of it even on the screen.

Cricket is a game that has evolved and developed since the eighteenth century, and I laugh when I hear all the pontificating about the game as it is today and about the introduction of Twenty20 and the amount of money that's being put into it, because I just think of the Regency. People don't generally realise that Beau Brummell, the famous Regency dandy who snubbed the Prince of Wales, actually became famous, not because of the cut of his neck-tie, but because he had been a magnificent cricketer. He was an Old Etonian and played cricket at school and went on to play, well, it wasn't professional cricket in those days but serious cricket and walked away from it, to everyone's distress, because of the corruption and gambling that were creeping into the game. Of course everything in the Regency was about gambling; it was a great age for losing your shirt and much the same applied to cricket. I suppose it was Victorian morality that changed all that.

Today we live in a great age of gambling, don't we? I mean, what do you think those bankers and stockbrokers and futures investors were doing if it wasn't gambling? And so there we are going back to massive amounts of money going into cricket and Twenty20 matches because they're quicker and you can get your fix quicker. No matter, it will still be cricket and I dare say that somewhere along the line it'll all have to be cleaned up and all the money will run out. But it still doesn't take away the joy that is cricket. I rather prefer my cricket nowadays at village level or at a match like this because you see more of the players and they're not celebrities. The extraordinary thing is that you have exactly the same set-up as there has always been: the large, burly village blacksmith hurling killing balls down the wicket only to have his wicket taken in turn by some quick schoolboy on holiday who hurtles down the wicket, lithe as you like. For me, as long as there is cricket, there will be English countryside.

There has been a rather delightful spin-off from my umpiring this match. Mark, who is very good company (when he's not deeply focused and serious, organising a cricket match) is an ex-member of the King's Troop Royal Horse Artillery whose barracks were in Ordnance Hill, just down the road from where I grew up in St John's Wood. When I was a child I stared at the horses and I suppose when I got a bit older, I stared at the soldiers. The regiment used to exercise on Wormwood Scrubs on certain days of the week and in order to get there would ride past my house and I would hear them early in the morning on summer days, the clack of the horses' hooves and sometimes the rumble of the guns when they were going out to practise with them. It must have been strange for my father who was a horse-gunner at the beginning of the First World War because my parents' bedroom actually overlooked the street and he would have been able to get out of bed and see them going past. If you have ever been at a country show and seen them performing a musical ride with the guns bouncing behind them, you'll know that their turn of speed and dexterity are amazing. The rear gunner, who's the one who is likely to get clouted by the pole that runs down the middle of the traces, wears this strange metal boot, curiously shaped to protect his leg, which you will see an example of if you look at the gunners' memorial at Hyde Park Corner. They seem to be a regiment that has woven in and out, not just of my dreams, but of my life for many years.

Anyway that's not really the point of my story. Mark came ostensibly to pick up some books that I had donated to a raffle and asked me, knowing that in my own small way I do judge hounds, if I would be interested in judging some bloodhounds and draghounds. Draghounds are hounds that are bred and trained for speed and follow a trail very fast across fell-type country. I said that I didn't know, but I might if I could manage the date, at which point he said, 'Oh, I think you'll manage the date, it's Peterborough Hound Show.' This hasn't happened yet so I can't tell you about it, only that I'm very excited indeed and feel very humble to be asked.

Peterborough is the doyen of hound judging, seconded, and I'll probably get shot for saying this, only by Lowther in the north. All the huntsmen in their finery bring their prize hounds to show in the show-ring and there are hounds of all shapes and sizes from every discipline of hunting. It is a great triumph for the hunting community that people are still breeding hounds and that they can show them and be rewarded for their efforts.

People have been breeding hounds since before the birth of Christ. The greyhound and indeed all the gazehounds, with the possible exception of the whippet, can trace their lineage back 4,000 years before Christ. Alexander of Macedon (Alexander the Great) travelled with his greyhounds in his efforts to conquer the world and took them over the mountain ranges into northern India, now Pakistan, and to this day coursing is the major sport in that part of the world. They have park coursing events rather as they do in Ireland and on an average day think nothing of having crowds of between 10,000 and 30,000.

The Romans imported hounds from Britain, most probably deerhounds and wolfhounds, all hair and ivory teeth and dark eyes. Somewhere in the Middle Ages the great black hound of St Hubert started to develop into what we now see as the standard hound, by way of the staghound, the buckhound and eventually the foxhound. There are centuries and centuries of pedigree in those hounds and, unlike most of the dogs shown at Crufts, they were bred to do what they do best, with the emphasis on their noses, stamina and running ability and so they have not become effete, distorted creatures like so many other breeds. When I was on the TV programme *Balderdash and Piffle* for the word 'dog', we filmed at Crufts and in one of the bits with the hounds the people round about were saying, 'You want to film that one, Clarissa, she's been entered.' By which they meant that she'd actually been hunted. One year a whippet won at Crufts and when the owner was asked why this particular animal hadn't been shown since it was a puppy she didn't answer, but my guess is that it had gone to do what all whippets do best, which was coursing.

I do have the most extraordinary life that even I in my most extravagant dreams never thought possible or that I would find myself judging at Peterborough. There is a bit in the AA's *Big Book* that refers to sobriety, saying that if we work our programme things will happen beyond our wildest dreams and I remember sniffing at this when I was fairly early into sobriety because when I got sober I really did believe that my life would be boring, dull and glum, but that it would be manageable. I can hear you laughing in the distance. Since I got sober my life has never been boring, dull and glum. It's been a whirlwind of different experiences and by and large things that I either enjoy at the time, or look back on with hindsight and see how they fit into the great jigsaw that is my life. But nobody could say that my life is remotely manageable. Everybody's dreams are different, in or out of recovery, and for some it's security, marriage, a family. For my part I have never had any real plans in the last twenty-two years and nor do I have any now. On those rare occasions when I did make plans, they have usually come crashing down in ruins around my ears. But you may remember if you read *Spilling the Beans* my mother's comment, 'Leave it to God, Clarissa – he has a better imagination than you have.' And certainly in my life this has been very true. Nobody else could have devised my path over the last twenty-two years, from finding Books for Cooks by accident to meeting Pat Llewellyn to *Two Fat Ladies* and onwards. People say to me, 'What next? What's left?' and I shrug my shoulders and say, 'Well, I don't know. I don't know if there's anything left really.' Stay home and write detective stories. And then out of the blue comes something like Peterborough or the Sandringham WI.

Asian beef salad

This recipe is dedicated to my friend and agent, Heather Holden-Brown, who I felt ought to have her own recipe as I designed one for her assistant Elly James in *Clarissa's Comfort Food*. Heather's birthday is in August. When I asked her what she would like me to do something with, she said, rare roast beef. As I eat a lot of rare roast beef, or indeed raw beef – I'm very fond of my carpaccio – this is a dish I make quite often at home.

Take 2 or 3 thin slices of rare roast beef or the equivalent of raw fillet steak, in which case cut it into thin slices, and lay the meat on a flat plate. If you are using raw meat, squeeze on some lime juice, say of half a lime at this stage. Pour over some olive oil and a dash of sesame oil and leave to stand for about 20 minutes.

a piece of ginger the size of your thumb
6 spring onions
1 red chilli
a packet of egg noodles
a packet of bean sprouts
soya sauce

Chop your ginger, your spring onions and your chilli, deseeding if you don't like it too hot, and fry these in a large pan or a wok in a little olive oil. Add the noodles. If these are dry you will need to boil them according to instructions first, otherwise just throw them in along with the bean sprouts. Cook all this together for a little while and add a good dash of soya sauce. Cut your meat into strips and throw it into the mixture, just really allowing it to heat through, or if you're using raw meat let it cook a little longer. If you're using cooked beef which has not yet had any lime juice, squeeze on some lime juice at this stage. If you want this as a cold dish, I would suggest that you use glass noodles and cook the meat separately and then lay it on top. However if you are having it as a hot dish, just mix everything together. Adjust the seasoning, adding a little more soya sauce if you like, perhaps a little more chilli sauce, or anything that suits your fancy and eat hot or cold.

September

Take the grease fat stag before the rut

It is curious that since my sexual dalliance behind the Speaker's Chair in the sixties – and I'm afraid I must inform you that nobody has stood up to be counted; it may be that the MP in question is dead or he's just keeping his head down – I have spent more time outside Parliament protesting or waving banners than I have ever spent inside it. I suppose, thinking about it, one of the reasons why I would have had no cause to do more than protest outside Parliament is that for the last twelve years we have had this particular Labour government who have had not one single policy that I could possibly agree with. This is not because I'm not a socialist; there are very often policies that run across the parties and indeed in Scotland I find myself agreeing with the Scottish socialists but not the Blair/Brown consortium. However, I was set to revisit Parliament because in very quick succession I found myself bidding at auctions for a couple of lunches in the House.

The first was at Otis Ferry's fundraiser to rebuild the South Shropshire Hunt kennels where he is joint master. Otis Ferry is a nice young man who only ever wanted to hunt with hounds and by dint of this particular government's attitude has found himself caught up in a protest when he and four friends managed to make a brilliant entry into the House of Commons during the hunting debate in 2004, thereby illustrating what a waste all the hundreds of thousands of pounds spent on security had been. If only Otis had read his history books and thrown the mace out of the window into the Thames, in which case Parliament is not deemed to be in session, how different things might have been. News of their protest went round the world. It didn't save us, but, God, it made us feel good on the day as we protesters all stood outside in Parliament Square. Anyway, the consequence for poor Otis is that he's been persecuted by the authorities ever since and the Health and Safety people said that he had to rebuild his kennels. I've been round his kennels and I must say I couldn't see anything wrong with them. Otis even ended up in prison as a result of an allegation that he had tried to suborn a witness in another case, a man who had numerous previous convictions for dishonesty and in whose police statement it actually said, 'When I said I was lying, I was lying.' All the charges against Otis have now been dropped but he missed the whole hunting season which was a great shame for a young man and his passion.

So I bid rather a lot of money to have lunch with Otis and Kate Hoey in the House of Commons. Kate Hoey is another of my heroines, who was the Sports Minister in Tony Blair's cabinet when she stood up for hunting, an action that brought her career as a cabinet minister to a premature conclusion. She is now the chairman of Countryside Alliance. Curious that she's the chairman and my friend Annie Mallalieu, a Labour peer, is the president so that if people start shouting, 'Oh, Tory toffs!' or whatever, with regard to hunting, they should bear that in mind. Kate is a very energetic and active hands-on chairman and it is a great pleasure to know her and so I was delighted by the thought of this particular lunch. It hasn't yet taken place but I'm sure we shall have a lovely day.

The other lunch I bought at the House of Commons was with Jim Paice, the shadow deputy Defra minister, of whom I had heard much good spoken, and I simply couldn't resist it because I was very interested to meet him. So I bid for it at the Game Conservancy dinner in Cambridgeshire at which I was speaking and acquired it for rather less money than I paid for the lunch with Otis and Kate Hoey.

Going into the House of Commons now is incredibly complicated. You have to go in through the main hall and you are stopped and they photograph your retinal image before they give you a pass. Fortunately they don't, unlike the airports, make you take your shoes off. All this seemed rather tiresome to me and smacked slightly of arrogance. If people want to get explosives into the House of Commons, they usually seem to do so: first Guy Fawkes and then the IRA. So far the Muslim fundamentalist terrorists have shown no signs of wanting to blow up the Houses of Parliament at all. Why would they? I should think the present government's far too nice to them.

Anyway, having walked miles across the Great Hall and up some fairly steep stairs, I was met by Jim Paice, who I found a delightful man; one of those extremely rare things in politics, an honest man. Of course he comes of farming stock and even to this day keeps a herd of Highland cattle just to remind himself of his roots. I suspect he thought that I had come to discuss hunting but in fact I wanted to talk to him about Section 36 of the Trade Descriptions Act which some of you may know is one of my great bugbears and concerns dishonest food labelling, where there is no indication at all as to the country of origin.

Section 36 is an appalling piece of legislation which says that a product may be named as coming from the place where it last underwent any process. Which means that you get Chilean salmon, smoked in Italy, sliced and packaged in Scotland and sold as Scottish smoked salmon. Or Chinese chicken breasts, fed on human excrement, brought into this country on the bone, sliced off the bone with a flick of the wrist and so you have British chicken. By the simple removal of this one section of legislation, you would stop all that. We had a surprisingly nice lunch. The food in the House of Commons has obviously improved over the years since I was last there. In this present Labour government and the ones before, the people who were put in charge of Defra or its predecessor MAFF were not country people, and knew nothing about farming, or food production and top of their agenda was that you could import food more cheaply than you could produce it. Why do I say that? Because when I was on the BBC's *Politics Show*, I asked Margaret Beckett why, when I was at one of the northern agricultural shows, the Defra stand carried no information about farming and food production and they told me, 'Oh, you can import it cheaper.' And Mrs Beckett replied, 'What idiot said that?' I said presumably somebody who was expressing the truth for once. Now, of course, everything's turned about and I doubt we'll be able to import food more cheaply, which is possibly one of the few good things that may come out of the current crisis and economic downturn that the world is experiencing.

I had not, for some reason, made the link that I was due shortly after this lunch to speak to the Conservative Ladies Association in Jim Paice's constituency which was organised by his delightful and very efficient wife, Ava. They very kindly invited me to stay with them for this speaking engagement and I was able to talk further about Section 36 and food labelling, which was most interesting because we were all singing from the same hymn sheet.

Some time later on, I received a telephone call from Jim Paice, saying that the Conservative Party were launching a campaign at the National Farmers' Union AGM against dishonest food labelling and would I be willing to record a video to be used as part of this campaign and as part of the website they were launching. At that time, I was in Leicestershire but naturally, like an old hunter hearing the horns and hounds in the distance, I turned round and got a train back to London, leaving my car behind, and recorded the video. I have to say that the young researchers in the shadow Defra department were extraordinarily good and efficient and I was most impressed by them. They had got together the most horrendous collection of mislabelled products.

The worst offender, I think, was Marks and Spencer who produced a corned beef and pickle bap which was wrapped in a packet with a Union Jack across the top and written along the bottom was, 'Britain's favourite food'. It was only with great difficulty and a magnifier that I managed to make out the very small print on the back which said, 'Made from beef from Marks and Spencer approved farms in Brazil', which is a terrifying thought given the consequences of chopping down the rainforests and global warming and everything else. Curiously, if they have to buy it abroad, I don't know why they don't buy it from Argentina, which was always the traditional source of corned beef for the British Isles. However when asked about this, Marks and Spencer replied that you couldn't make corned beef in Britain, which is a load of rubbish because I actually make it in my own kitchen at home sometimes, just for the fun of it.

Another example of mislabelling was 'Made with either British or Brazilian chickens' and there was much more along similar lines. I suppose it was a marginal improvement on Section 36, in that somewhere on the back of the packaging you could, if your eyesight was good enough or you had a magnifying glass in the supermarket, read where it came from.

Not long after my lunch with Jim Paice, I went to the forty-ninth birthday party of my friend Jan McCourt who farms and fattens rare-breed beef and pork and lamb in Cold Overton on the Rutland/Leicestershire border. He said everybody was having fiftieth birthday parties so he was going to have a forty-ninth and was combining this with one of his open days so that he could use the tentage for the party. It is because of Jan that I became so involved with the campaign to register the Melton Mowbray pork pie process and also the Melton Mowbray Food Festival, as he introduced me to its founder, Matthew O'Callaghan.

The meat Jan produces (and you can buy it at Borough Market if you can't visit his shop) is of excellent quality. He is one of the two people in the British Isles from whom I regularly buy pork because the meat is properly fattened, has a nice covering of fat and tastes absolutely delicious. He also does very good beef and Jacob sheep of all things. I never really thought that Jacob sheep were for eating but actually they are really tasty. Jan used to be a city financier, long before it was unfashionable to be so, and after being made redundant many years ago he decided to follow his dream to be a farmer and raise proper meat. It was Jan who catered my sixtieth birthday party, which was a great success, and supplied all the steaks. The menu for each table showed, not only the type of beast it was, but also its ear tag number, its age, when it had been killed and how long it had been hung. They also have a catering van emblazoned with the name Northfield Farm that they take to shows from which they sell the best ever hamburgers and sausages and bacon.

The open day was great fun. Within the confines of the farm buildings, there is not only the farm shop, but also an extremely good wine shop run by a man called Patrick Whenham-Bossy who used to be the chief sommelier of Hambleton Hall. There is a furniture restorer too, from whom I have bought and ordered many interesting pieces of furniture over the years. Sadly, now he is just doing restoring but I'm sure if you ask him nicely he will make something for you. Altogether it was a most enjoyable event, as his open days always are, with hawks on display, food to eat, and stalls selling chocolates and home-made cakes and macaroons and various artefacts. And of course I sat there signing books and chatting happily to people. If you want to find out when the next one is, go on to the Northfield Farm website.

The birthday party was the next day, for which Jan had found this extraordinarily good jazz band, TJs. I'm a great fan of jazz and in the days when Clive, the love of my life, and I were together we used to go to the 100 Club almost every week to hear jazz. The 100 Club is at 100 Oxford Street and you heard all the greats there: Acker Bilk, Humphrey Lyttelton, Kenny Ball and the like. As a result I'm something of an aficionado and tend to be surprised at how much bad jazz there is around the country, but this band was excellent and had a really good clarinettist of a calibre I haven't heard for a long time.

Someone I was delighted to meet at the open day and of course at the party was Willie Robson who was there with his wife, Daphne. Willie is a leading authority on British bees and runs the Chain Bridge Honey Farm on the Northumbrian border; he takes his bees all over that part of the north of England and is particularly noted for his heather honey. He's one of the very few people who sells heather honey in the comb. I know this because my butcher Colin Peat stocks it and it's absolutely delicious.

The farm also makes various polishes and ointments from the beeswax. I can vouch for their Propolis cream which is made from a wax-like substance produced by bees; a few years ago I had a very nasty horsefly bite on my forehead, slightly my fault because I swatted the horsefly against my forehead and it bit me viciously as it died. The wound refused to heal up and I had this great gaping hole in my forehead until Jan gave me a pot of this Propolis ointment; after about two or three days the hole started closing up and finally healed over completely and now you can't see a mark at all.

Bees have always fascinated me. Their whole life-cycle is really nature red in tooth and claw because the worker bees work until their wings wear out, at which point the wings are removed by the soldier bees so that they can fly no more and they die. Over the years I have had a number of friends who have kept bees in various parts of the country, one of them in Richmond Park, in the grounds of the Royal Ballet School. Richmond Park is much sought after as a venue for hives among London beekeepers because as an enclosed royal park since the reign of Charles I it has never been ploughed or sown or sprayed and so any honey gathered there can be described as organic.

My friend said the only thing they forget is the picnickers and she showed me a comb of honey that was the most vivid, bright pink and smelled horribly of various synthetic substances and she said, 'I think the bees had found their way into a bottle of cherryade that had been left behind by the picnickers.' And I realised she was absolutely right, it was the same colour and smell as the cherryade I used to drink when I was young. But it was still theoretically organic. This same beekeeper told me a lovely story of one day when her husband was walking along Harley Street and a leading practitioner, who was also a beekeeper, flung up his window in his excitement at seeing him and called, 'James, James, come in quick, come and see my Circassian virgins,' at which a great many passing Arabs screeched to a halt and stared hungrily at the window. He was of course talking about imported queens. A lot of bee stock is imported, which is not necessarily a good thing because the native British bee has been under attack for as long as I can remember, more from the importation of disease that comes in with foreign bees than from the grey squirrel syndrome.

Until I tasted Willie Robson's honey, I'd actually forgotten that I like honey because so much of the stuff you get now is rather watery and thin, since the huge, great crops of rape around the country that the bees feed on don't produce very pleasant honey at all. Bees can be kept in all sorts of strange and wonderful places. If you sit at dusk and look patiently up at the roof of Harrods, you will see bees returning to their hives there from the various London parks and gardens where they have been feeding and pollinating.

My friend Olga Romanoff tells the story of her house, Provender, in Kent, where bees were forever coming down the chimney. Olga's mother was a somewhat eccentric person and when she was still alive and I saw these little bowls of sugary water (as I now know they were) sitting around in the various fireplaces, I was worried to ask her what they were for in case she might tell me they were for feeding fairies or something. Then I saw some bees feeding at these shallow dishes and I asked about them and it emerged that in the 1890s or so some workmen going up into the roof to do some structural work came across this huge, white, throbbing, buzzing object and ran away screaming, thinking it was some sort of supernatural phenomenon. When they were persuaded to go back they discovered that it was a huge, natural hive that the bees had made, and in fact I believe they took something like half a tonne of honey out of it. These natural hives are not uncommon. Sometimes they get so big that they fall through the roof and damage buildings. There's one in the roof of the manor house where I live and the bees come down the chimney there.

Bees have been around mankind for years; just look at the various primitive tribes who still go out and harvest the honey from wild bees by climbing up cliff faces and trees at some danger to themselves in order to get the delicious substance that is honey. Before the growth and industrialisation of sugar cane, honey was really one of the very few sweeteners in the world. At the beginning of the nineteenth century the old straw bee skeps, a sort of early hive, which were unsatisfactory in that they led to the growth of disease and bees being destroyed when the honey was taken, were replaced by hives very much as we know them now, with the structure for bees to land on and the hole for bees to go in and the removable stretchers to take the cone honey away from the hive.

The bee is going through a bad time at the moment. All over the world, bee colonies are collapsing and dying and of course the bee is very valuable, not just for its production of honey, but also for pollination. Bees are the most important pollinators in the agricultural world, pollinating fruit crops, rape crops, flowers and anything you can think of that needs cross-pollinating, and so they need to be encouraged.

The trouble is that the bee is quintessentially a wild animal. It lives adjacent to us rather than with us and Willie Robson made the point that an awful lot of people who are now going into beekeeping thinking it's easy, really don't know how to look after their bees. It's important that the hives are kept clean, that the bees are properly cared for and fed in the winter and that when they're moved to follow whatever crop is flowering at the time, they're moved gently and quietly to ensure that they don't get stressed.

A lot of bee colonies are being killed by the Vero mite which is a minuscule little creature that attacks bees and decimates the colonies; this again emphasises the necessity of keeping everything around the hive clean and sanitised. But now we're also finding that there is a growth in bee viruses, which nobody really understands. In America, where bees are moved thousands of miles from one end of the country to the other in order to feed them all the year round, they're suffering a very bad outbreak of colony collapse, with the bees becoming distressed and dying. Common sense seems to me to indicate that this is the result of stress, rather than a reaction to the forces of global warming as some think, because bees are being asked to behave in a manner that they would never do in their natural habitat. The bee is taken from its environment, from pastures it knows, to a different countryside with a different climate and expected to start working again. It's surely not beyond the wit of man to be able to provide bees that will pollinate in their own area without carting them across the nation. This current practice smacks to me of greed, pure and simple.

Willie Robson's bees, on the other hand, don't travel very far and his 1,800 hives feed on the local rape, the borage and heather and (here I suppose lies another difference) go peacefully into hibernation for the winter. And did you know that apparently if you eat honey from the area where you live it will remove any danger of hay fever, sadly not something I can attest to because I never stay in one place long enough. Bees are worth about £30 million in pollination activities to the British economy, and about the same again in honey and wax products. They are a valuable asset and it would be a terrible thing if we were to lose them.

Later in September a friend and I travelled to the Nare Hotel in the Roseland in Cornwall, whose charming owner Toby had given me his card at the Royal Cornwall Show in June. In the Blair years he had refused to let rooms to Mr Blair, which immediately endeared him to me, and he asked me to come and visit his hotel, which he had taken over from his grandmother. I decided that this sounded exactly what I needed. The hotel is in the most perfect position overlooking the long white beach in the Roseland peninsula, an extraordinarily lush and beautiful area, and it has an indoor swimming pool as well as an outdoor one and a hot-tub. I have to say that I swam every day. It also has tennis courts and is incredibly genial and friendly and the food was very good, the lobster in particular. If you had good enough eyesight, which by that time of the year I didn't, you could see the lobster pots in the bay in front of the hotel where quite a lot of the fish were caught too.

The church of St Just in Roseland which we went to visit is very curious because the church lies by the water, down quite a steep hill from the road, and around it, on a higher level, is the churchyard. Its elevated position is a result of the fact that everybody believed that at the last trump they would all rise to heavenly glory together and they didn't want to be separated from their families so they were buried on top of each other, thereby artificially raising the height of the whole churchyard. If you walk along row upon row of little stones, identifying the family groups, it's an attractive and peaceful place and I would have thought that when the last trump came they probably turned round and said, 'Well actually we'd rather stay here because Paradise couldn't be better than this.'

Toby's grandmother, after a life in hoteliering, had opened this hotel as her retirement project, but had recently given it over to him. She lived just opposite the hotel and would come across with her funny little Tibetan spaniel every day and had her own table for dinner where she could keep an eye on things. She was the most charming woman and when my friend pointed out that it was difficult for me to get down to the beach, because my foot was particularly bad at the time, she said, 'I will take you in my golf buggy.' And so into the golf buggy I got, with the little spaniel in his basket on the back, and off we set. For various reasons we got on to the beach as the tide was coming in and she said to me, 'The thing to do when you get to the bottom of the ramp is not to stop, otherwise you may sink.' So we hit the beach running and kept going; in fact at one point two of the wheels went over a rock and I found myself leaning out to balance the vehicle as if I were sailing. Some man said, 'What is this? Is it some sort of obscure, dangerous off-roading?' and we both giggled like children and shot off along the sand and back again. Altogether it was a delightful interlude, a very jolly and much needed holiday and God was kind and the weather was perfect.

To get to the Roseland, you either go to Truro and down on the King Harry Ferry to St Mawes or you drive the long way round by road. Cornwall is full of ferries and I used to love the King Harry Ferry when I was a child. It chunters up and down, doesn't take very long and gives you a perfect view of the inlet and its shipping. I adore ferries; they sort of stop the world for those ten or fifteen minutes that it takes you to get on to the ferry, cross the inlet and get off again. When I was young, the only way across the Humber was by ferry because they hadn't built the Humber Bridge and indeed Queen Margaret's ferry went backward and forward across the Firth of Forth. Such crossings always seemed a huge adventure.

Thinking of ferries reminds me of a rather scandalous story that I told my friend as we were belting across on the King Harry Ferry. Photographs were found of the late Margaret, Duchess of Argyll, with what was referred to as 'the headless man', because his head was out of the picture, to whom she was giving a blow-job. This was regarded as deeply shocking and much speculation took place as to the identity of the headless man. The late Douglas Fairbanks Junior, who was supposed to be one of the contenders, went into chambers with the judge and the two barristers during the subsequent divorce trial brought by her husband, the 11th Duke, to drop his trousers and prove quite definitively that he wasn't the man. One doesn't know how he was able to prove it but one can speculate. Anyway, this particular scandal was plastered over every newspaper in the kingdom, or at least most of them.

In those days, the 1960s, *The Times* was a terribly respectable newspaper and didn't stoop to such tittle-tattle. Its front page was covered with the lists of hatched, matched and despatched – births, deaths and marriages – and the back page displayed artistic photographs of scenery, of mountains or new buildings in towns or whatever. The paper's only comment on the Argyll scandal was a photograph on the back page of Inveraray Pier with the view looking out across the loch and to the side of the picture the sign for the ferry boat that shuttled to and fro, which said very clearly: *Queue here for the Duchess of Argyll.*

My mother could not abide Margaret Argyll who was a contemporary of hers, and always referred to her as 'that Maggie Whigham'. I have on my bookshelves the Duchess of Argyll's cookery book, which is the most perfect historic document of English cookery in the 1930s, and she quite clearly never moved on. Bizarrely, she says that when she was married to her first husband, Charles Sweeney, they had really disastrous dinner parties because they invited their friends but when she was married to Ian Argyll everything changed because they had these wonderful dinner parties where their guests were all sorts of celebrities and people like Prince Philip. It is the most teeth-gritting book and I can see why my mother wasn't fond of her. When she married the Duke of Argyll she was a very rich woman and she poured some of her substantial fortune into Inveraray Castle, the Argyll seat on the shores of Loch Fyne. However when the divorce came, because under Scottish law the home of a clan laird is an incorporeal hereditament as it's called up here, or an heirloom as it's called down south, she was unable to retrieve her money and eventually died in some poverty, having had to move out of her suite in the Dorchester and into the Cumberland Hotel. I believe – oh, what a dreadful thought – that she was unable to afford caviar on a daily basis. I'm not sure why she didn't move into one of the many hundreds of rooms at Belvoir Castle where her daughter was the Duchess of Rutland, but perhaps there was a family rift.

In younger, happier days, September would have seen the start of cubbing, or autumn hunting, as the Masters of Foxhounds Association told us that we had to call it. It was that time of year when the young hounds were entered into the field for the first time, and one would get up incredibly early in the morning, at first light, so that they could go and chase the young foxes who had been born in the spring of the year and were fully grown cubs. The purpose of this exercise was to give the young hounds some idea of scent and to scatter the young cubs because if foxes are left to live in packs they become very different, more competently aggressive creatures. During the last foot and mouth epidemic, when there was no hunting and not much movement on the land, a friend of mine who was a sheep farmer came out at night because he heard a commotion and found six foxes attacking one lamb. One fox is quite sufficient to kill a lamb; six foxes will kill you as well. But it was a happy time; there was no need for formal clothes and you went out on your horse which was still slightly full of summer grass and was having its first exercise of the autumn. I recollect sitting around copses and fields of standing crops, banging my whip against my boot or against the flap of my sandal just to make a noise to alert the young foxes. The hounds bounced around, ran in and out of the cover and didn't really know what they were doing, and it was nice to see all the friends that one hadn't perhaps seen during the summer until the hunting season re-started.

Being in Cornwall reminded me of this and brought back an occasion when I went out with friends with the Fourborough Hunt and was offered jam sandwiches by a small, blonde child who was terribly excited because one of the young foxes came out of cover right in front of us, with not a hound in sight. She was delighted at this and was very determined, at the age of four, that the next time she came she would bring her pony. Now of course we are restricted to a duster and an aniseed trail.

A few years ago, before the hunting ban, I received an

invitation to open Bugthorpe Show in the East Riding of Yorkshire. It was the most charming letter, and you could hear the Yorkshire accent in the writing: 'Dear Clarissa, If we may be so bold, we would like to ask you to open Bugthorpe Show. It is not a very big show but you would eat your traditional roast beef and Yorkshire pudding to the mellifluous sounds of our local brass band. 'Tis not a very big band but it's very mellifluous. Lest you should lose popularity in Yorkshire we would not ask you to judge cakes and jams, we'd leave that to Lady Halifax, but we would like to ask you to open the show and present prizes. Do hope you can come.'

How could you resist a letter like that? So I went and Bugthorpe Show was indeed a very small show, but quite delightful. Having looked through *The Good Pub Guide* for somewhere to stay, I found a pub that mentioned hunting and foxes and suchlike, I think three or four times on the page, so I decided it sounded like my sort of place and I booked myself a room.

I drove across the Trough of Boland from Cheshire to Yorkshire on the most beautiful day, with the roof of my car down, feeling at great peace with the world. And sure enough I hadn't been in the pub more than about ten minutes when somebody came up to me and said, 'Hounds are meeting across at the hall at six o'clock tomorrow morning, do come.' So I went and spent this lovely morning. I often think of it when Richard Burge, who was the previous chief executive of the Countryside Alliance, organised a women's vigil because he said that he wanted the world to see the softer face of hunting and the Bedale, which was the hunt in question where I went cubbing, was known in my generation for the toughness of its female riders who were extremely hard-bitten. I remember saying to him, 'Well, for heaven's sake, don't put the Bedale ladies in the front row.'

All that excellent lobster I'd eaten in Cornwall, both at Rick Stein's and at the Nare, led me to thinking about crayfish. I have this mind that hops around, you see. Our rivers used to be full of native crayfish. When I was a child we used to catch them with bits of old meat, then boil them up and they were quite delicious. Sadly, somewhere along the way somebody imported the sentinel crayfish from America which, like the grey squirrel, is bigger, more aggressive and easier to rear and these were to be bred for the market. Unfortunately they escaped and, as with the grey squirrel, wiped out an awful lot of our native crayfish. They are sunny-looking creatures, the sentinel, very red with huge claws. After we'd written *A Greener Life*, Johnny Scott and I went to a house in north London to give an interview to a woman journalist who was endeavouring to live a greener life. She had chickens in an Eglu and was growing vegetables in her garden and so forth. She kept some sentinel crayfish in a bowl and Johnny tried to pick one up and missed. You pick up any members of the crayfish or lobster family from the back behind the head so that they can't nip you but Johnny's aim was poor and he got very badly nipped and the claws drew blood. So he spent the entire interview with his hand behind his back.

Interestingly, the fortunes of the sentinel crayfish have changed due to the influx of Polish workers who are used to living off the land. They have wiped out the sentinel crayfish which they've fished for on the Lee and the other rivers that run round London with great gusto, taken them home and had crayfish suppers, so that now there may be a chance for our native crayfish to stage a resurgence. If they've been so successful, it does raise the question as to whether a grey squirrel cull might be equally successful.

From crayfish my mind hopped to thinking of Sweden. One of my best friends, Carin, is Swedish. I met her in London and sadly some years ago she moved to southern Spain and is now one of the 55,000 Swedes who live on the Costa del Sol because they want the sun. One is sometimes tempted to think that the entire Viking migrations, especially to the Mediterranean, were really in search of the sun rather than loot and plunder. Anyway, she also has a house in Sweden where she spends the summer. September is the time for crayfish and the Swedes have parties at the drop of a hat for any sort of reason but their crayfish parties are legendary. You have a huge bowl of cooked crayfish and lots of mayonnaise and some salad and of course lots and lots of schnapps and everybody has a lovely time. The crayfish are quite delicious and as I've given up the schnapps, obviously I get rather more crayfish than a lot of people.

Thinking of the Swedes and parties leads me on to the surströmming party season. Surströmming is something that is peculiar to northern Sweden and is literally translated as rotten herring. It dates back to the early nineteenth century when some southern Swedes had been fishing for herring in the northern waters and had had insufficient salt to pack the herring with and the fish started to deteriorate, so they sold the barrels to the northern Swedes. When they went back the following year, slightly apprehensive as to how they would be received because of the bad fish they had sold, they were welcomed by the northern Swedes who said, 'We don't want these perfect herrings, we want more of what you sold us last year, it was absolutely magic.' And so surströmming was born. The late Alan Davidson in his *North Atlantic Seafood* book says that when you take the lid off a barrel of surströmming the seagulls fall from the sky at the stench, and certainly it is a very peculiar thing. It shimmers on the plate and there's a sort of slight haze over it; the smell is quite extraordinary and revolting but it gives the Swedes a perfect excuse to drink huge quantities of schnapps and prove how brave they are by eating the surströmming. People swear to me that they actually like it. Having only come across it in recovery, I've been very bold and tried it, but I can't say that it did anything for me.

Carin once gave me a tin of surströmming, a very beautiful tin, engraved with the Swedish coat of arms and I put it on the shelf as a talking point in my sitting room. I noticed that the tin was getting bigger and sort of seemed to be swelling so the next time Carin came to see me I said, 'Look at that tin! It's beginning to swell.' And she said, 'You must get rid of it, or it will explode and you'll have to vacate your flat if that happens because it will make such a horrible mess.' So I said, 'Oh, thank you very much.' I put it straight into the dustbin. When I got home on dustbin day the entire street on which I lived smelled as though the drains had been blocked incredibly badly for about six months and my neighbours told me, 'We can't understand what this horrible smell is. We've called the council and they've said there's nothing they can do.' And then it dawned on me with horror that refuse lorries have crushers and one of the prongs must have gone through my surströmming tin, so I slunk quietly to my flat and shut the door.

This whole question of semi-rotten food is quite fascinating. I suppose that it was simply a different flavour in historic times. In Iceland, for instance, they have a most disgusting dish of shark that has been buried in the permafrost until it starts to rot, and I have to tell you that you really don't want to try it.

It stays in your nasal hairs for up to three days if not more. And in our own Scotland, in the Western Isles, we have the guga. I'm one of the few people outside the islands ever to have been privileged to eat guga.

My friend Sue Lawrence, the Scottish food writer, to whose dinner parties I accept invitations with alacrity and starve for several days beforehand because she's such a brilliant cook, said to me when she was writing her book, *A Cook's Tour of Scotland*, that she had been given a guga and would I like to go round and eat it. I thought I ought to out of friendship. The guga is a gannet that has been preserved or semi-preserved in salt. The men of Ness on Lewis still have a licence to harvest gannet and this is an annual tradition in the autumn. The gannet is not something one would rush to eat anyway, I suspect, but certainly not after it's been preserved in salt for six months or so. Anyway you could smell it as soon as you walked into Sue's house even though she had been rinsing it in cold running water for most of the day. And then we cooked it. Apparently it is not cooked in a complicated manner but just boiled. It looked like something out of a horror movie. It most resembled a grey dishcloth with big webbed seabird feet.

Also present to eat this delicacy were Linda Dick, who raises the most brilliant chickens and this was of course poultry of a sort, and Maxine Stuart, Sue's editor. Most people in the Western Isles don't drink alcohol because they're Wee Frees and so drink milk. The others drank whisky with it but I followed tradition with milk and it took an enormous amount of willpower not to rush to the nearest sink. It was excruciatingly horrible, one of the most disgusting things I've ever eaten, even more horrible than the Icelandic shark in the permafrost, but it did give me the answer to the question that I'm frequently asked, which is what is the most revolting thing I've ever eaten. We all tried desperately to imagine why it was a delicacy and while there's no doubt that there wasn't a lot else to eat out there, why this?

I discovered the next morning. There was not much in the way of vegetation growing in the Western Isles and the population suffered from intense constipation or, as we are supposed to call it now, slow digestive tract. The amount of bicarbonate of soda that is still shipped up that way has nothing whatsoever to do with their baking prowess. I remember reading an eighteenth-century account by somebody who had been fed some seabird's eggs that had been preserved for six months and had remarked rather dryly that they were welcome loosening. This no doubt is why they eat preserved guga.

I was terribly impressed with Sweden on my first visit there ten years ago. Among other things they grow the most delicious potatoes which you buy in the supermarkets and they taste like real potatoes. The same is true of all their vegetables. And their traceability is second to none, even in supermarkets – although there's nowhere much else to shop than supermarkets. Every product has a number and you can get a book from the government or go on the government website and check the number and it will tell you what farm the particular product comes from. Some of the meat packets even have a picture of the farmer on them alongside the number and you can be quite certain that they will be the genuine article, unlike some supermarket advertisements in this country where they show you pictures of supposed farmers and say that this is who supplies the produce in question. There was an example in a local supermarket where I live, with meat displaying a picture of a man who was supposed to be a sheep farmer but everybody in East Lothian knew that he was the local dustman.

In Sweden they also have all sorts of different milk products that we don't have here, such as the most delicious speciality called long milk which is rather like a sort of runny yoghurt. When you lift the spoon from it there are trailing strands beneath and this is apparently because the cows have been eating camomile, which has this particular effect on the milk. Carin and I went to a place called Jou, where they harvest or fish for char which live in the huge inland sea up there and smoke them over juniper bushes in the open. You go along and buy your char to take home or you sit and eat it at one of the little cafés and it is, again, yummy – really quite special.

On the way to Jou, we visited a large castle begun in the Middle Ages called Läckö Slott, where on the lake in front of the castle families happily pedalled around in giant pedalos in the shape of swans. We arrived rather late as Carin had underestimated the time it would take us to get there, and when we went into the restaurant, the only thing left was some fish and I thought, Oh dear, this late it's going to be really past its sell-by date – not very nice. I mean most of the food in National Trust houses in the British Isles ain't wonderful. But it was completely worthy of a top restaurant. Inside the castle they had an exhibition of hunting over the centuries and a room full of pelts from animals that had been hunted, for children to feel and roll around on to understand the natures of different furs, and I just thought, Imagine the furore if you tried to do that in the UK.

One thing that struck me was the most amazing wall decoration in black and white sections, which was made from badger pelt. The Swedes hunt badgers with dogs which I imagine are similar to the Dandie Dinmont or the dachshund which were originally bred for badger hunting. We have too many badgers in the British

Isles. It brings to mind that rather silly joke about Lord Boothby on his deathbed, saying to his friends, 'I don't understand it, you know, when I brought in my buggers bill, the House of Lords was packed, but the moment I brought in my badger protection bill there was almost nobody there.' And his friends said to him, 'Not a lot of badgers in the House of Lords.' Badger numbers got so out of hand in Scotland at one point that if you were driving along a country lane at night the first car hit the rabbit and the second car hit the badger that had run into the road to eat it because there were so many badgers that they were starving; you just prayed that you were the first car because a big badger can make an awful dent in your car.

A badger is a dangerous quarry because it will rush at the pursuer and clamp its jaws on to his leg or whatever part of his anatomy it can reach and will not let go until it hears the bones crack, which is why in Sweden hunters wore specially made boots with either eggshells and/or clinkers inside a double lining so that the badger would hear the clinkers or the eggshells crack and would then let go. When I was young, the West Country pubs used to sell badger ham which would sit on the bar like a *jamón ibérico* in a tapas bar in Spain, and you would buy slices off it, and it was extremely good. It was very much a country people's tradition and those who have eaten badger fillet cooked on the barbecue tell me that it is quite delicious and tastes like young wild boar.

The Swedes don't suffer from the odious sentimentality about animals that we British seem to indulge in, nor our unwillingness to recognise that wildlife needs to be culled. They're totally pragmatic and they control their wildlife. Anybody who's lived in an area that's predated by deer knows how much damage they can do to your garden let alone the crops. There is an enormous quantity of deer of all sorts in Sweden, from fallow right through to the giant moose and the Swedes eat a great deal of venison, which is readily available in the shops. They know that with a proliferation of deer comes the deer tick which when it bites you causes a very nasty illness called Lyme disease which can make you very ill and even kill you, so in Sweden it's quite commonplace to have preventive injections against it because the Swedes take to the woods in the summer. Every Swede who lives in a town has a little bothy out in the countryside where they go for the light nights and the month of August – a month that is particularly bad for deer ticks. They take their deer injections and learn to shoot deer and cull them rigorously, with permits allowing a specific number to be shot. Thus everything is kept under control.

Sweden is a huge country, fairly sparsely populated and abounding with lakes, which of course mean fish to me, and one of the great delights in Sweden is to go pike fishing on the lake. There are masses of pike in the lakes and it is the case once again that if you don't remove the pike you won't have much else in the lake. The only trouble is that when I've been fishing in Sweden, because my friend only goes in the summer, there have been long, hot days when the pikes stay down in the cool at the bottom and I spend a very frustrating time trying to catch them and just when I am about to go home having disentangled myself yet again from my pike lure, I finally start catching pike. Pike is even sold on fishmongers' slabs in Sweden, something you never see over here. All our pike, as far as I understand it, is exported to France, which is a great pity because it really is the most delicious of fish.

There is a very good restaurant called Clos du Marquis, just outside Stockbridge, run by an enchanting little French friend of mine called Germain. He asks all the keepers in the Test Valley and its tributaries to bring him their pike which he'll buy from them when they're clearing out the rivers, and with which he produces the most exquisite dishes, among them a pike mousse with a tiny monkfish liver embedded in the centre. You can't buy monkfish liver, as fishermen just throw it away, so you have to ask for it specially, but it is wonderfully rich and better really than the best of foie gras.

That was a good old rifle in the drawer, wasn't it? How I got from crayfish via everything else to monkfish liver is slightly beyond even my mindset, but I do recommend monkfish liver to you. If you're lucky enough to have a fishmonger, ask him for it because it is the most delicious thing to eat. Going back to pike, I remember when Johnny and I were filmed fishing in Northern Ireland out on Lough Erne and caught a pike which I filleted and made into ceviche, which is raw fish cooked in lemon juice, and everybody said, Oh, pike is so difficult to fillet. Not if you've tried your hand at flying fish, it's not. They have the same tripartate bone structure and when I was in the West Indies I used to go down to the fish markets and watch the old fishwives filleting the flying fish and asked them to teach me. It's not easy to fillet a flying fish but once you've mastered it, boy, is a pike a doddle.

The end of September sees one of the most delightful events of the country show year, the Hampshire Sportsman's Day, held at the Tichborne Estate in Hampshire. You may have heard of the curious case of the Tichborne claimant which was one of the causes célèbres of the Victorian legal system where the heir to the Tichborne fortune had disappeared to Australia and some years later a man re-emerged from Australia to claim his estate. A huge court case followed to discover whether he was or was not the genuine Tichborne claimant. Eventually the court found against him because when asked where in the confines of Harrow School the headmaster's study was off the quadrangle, he didn't know what a quadrangle was. It was a curious case, although it's never much spoken of because both the Tichborne heir and the claimant had a penis that drew back into his body rather like a horse. It's strange to think there should have been two men sharing a tent in the goldfields of Australia both with this particular unusual physical deformity, but so be it.

Anyway the estate remained in the family, having been inherited by the missing heir's younger brother, and this delightful place is host to this little one-day country fair. There's no tat, and no stalls that have been let in just to raise money. The Hampshire Hunt is there selling bits and pieces, and every year I buy matchboxes for the kitchen with pictures of hounds in the snow. The food is always good at the show. This time I had some truly delicious venison sausages, although I'm not a great fan of venison sausages, which had been made by Richard Wills and his wife from deer shot on their local estate in Hampshire.

One year I bought at auction a day's ferreting with Robinson's, the excellent butchers in Stockbridge. When I was younger, it used to be that butchers were also graziers in that they grazed or fattened stock, and a lot of them had their own abattoirs too so that the distance the animals had to travel from field to slab was minimal and all the better for that. Good butchers who sell game will often go out and catch their own rabbits. Rabbits are a nuisance, and being half Australian I feel no affection for them. The depredations that they committed on that continent are legendary. In an effort to keep the rabbits in one half of the country from getting into the western half where there were none, an immense rabbit-proof fence was built in the early

1900s right the way down the centre of Australia. And it was the Australian government that ordered the introduction of myxomatosis in 1950 to try to cut back the rabbit population. Those of us who were young in the fifties and early sixties will remember all too well the horrors when the British government released the disease into the rabbit population here and how you would always have to take a stick on a walk because you would find diseased rabbits lying around waiting to die, and you'd put them out of their misery.

Every landslide you hear about on the railway lines, which holds up train efficiency, is caused by rabbits burrowing into the bank. And an awful lot of building collapses are caused by rabbits under-burrowing. On the one hand they're a dangerous, noxious nuisance – a vermin – but on the other hand, if properly handled, they're very useful in supplying protein into the food system. Up until the mid-eighteenth century, rabbits were a delicate creature kept in warrens. They were valuable and in Norman times the proud and wealthy Warrenne family gained much of their wealth as well as their name from being the royal warreners. In Scotland the word is warrender. As recently as the Second World War there were still working warrens, the biggest being at Thaxstead in Essex which covered a square mile. One of the last working warrens was at Highclere in Berkshire and when I was shooting at Conholt, I had the most enchanting loader called Basil, whose father had been gamekeeper at Highclere. He told me he remembered as a boy that in the spring there would be these big buck rabbits running around in the walled vegetable garden, waiting to be introduced into the warren to improve the breeding stock. They'd usually been brought over from East Anglia. Rabbits fight like mad so there must have been some mighty battles to establish the new breeding stock.

Before the war rabbits were an extraordinarily useful part of the food chain. Wales used to send a whole trainload of rabbits each week up to the London markets and the fur trade and the glue trade dealt very heavily in rabbits; the reject from the fur traders was something like a million rabbit guts a month, showing how much rabbit fur actually went into the clothing market. Nowadays we import most of our rabbits from China, where God knows what they're fed on, or from France which are rabbits reared for the pot and we ignore the huge source of wild food that is out there waiting for us. A friend of mine whose father was a butcher said he used to go out and catch rabbits and at that time Leadenhall Market in the City of London sold a beam of rabbits a week, which is 1,000 rabbits a week. My generation with its memories of the myxomatosis epidemic has aged or passed on so I don't understand why these days when everybody's looking for leaner, healthier meat, wild rabbit is not on every menu. When I was at school, chicken was a luxury and we used to get dishes of what was supposed to be chicken although everybody knew it was in fact rabbit, and none the worse for that.

Those butchers who do sell rabbits – my own Colin Peat in Haddington, Robinson's and many others – say that they have no difficulty in selling them. If you are afraid that rabbit might be too gamey, let me assure you that it isn't a gamey meat, even wild rabbit. I don't think a butcher would be selling an old buck, but if you do catch one all you have to do is soak it in milk overnight to take out the strong flavour. And the best way to catch rabbits is with ferrets because if you shoot them you're likely to damage the flesh, or else you might miss or injure them, whereas if a ferret drives them out of the burrow into a net, and the man waiting above pulls their neck and breaks it, the rabbits will die quickly and cleanly.

Ferrets are the most extraordinary creatures. They're a member of the Mustelidae family with all that implies in terms of rather rank smells, especially the males, the hobs, but they make very good pets. In 2000 they were described as the pet of the millennium and they have a huge following in America where there are companies that sell toy castles for your ferrets to play in, swings for them to swing on and all sorts of other delights. They also sell costumes to dress up your ferret in, the most popular, I believe, being Bugs Bunny. I even came across an article in one of the magazines written by a psychologist about what to do when your ferret bites you, the answer being that you sit in a dark room with your ferret and talk to it and if it wants to, let it bite you again. Ferrets can give very nasty bites indeed so it's not advice I would be willing to follow. Ferrets need attention like any animal and so the more you handle or stroke your ferret, the happier it will be and the less likely to bite.

When I was young, ferreting was fraught with the peril of losing your ferret because it would go down a hole and it might kill a rabbit underground, have a lovely feast and go to sleep, at which point you would have to start digging to retrieve your ferret. Either that or sit for long hours and wait for it to come out. Now you can buy little sonar beepers that you put round the ferret's neck and you can track where they are so if you do have to dig them out you know exactly where to dig. Ferrets are thought to be native to central Europe and have been with us for a very long time. There are references in ancient Greek literature and plays to ferrets that even suggest a recipe for ferret pie – although I think that's some sort of bad joke, because I don't think you'd actually want to eat a ferret. There is a lovely medieval illustration from the Luttrell Psalter which shows men with ferrets catching rabbits, presumably in the wonderful warrens of the day, and apart from the clothes and the open hill, not a lot has changed. Ferrets are also very good for ratting. Put a ferret into a rat hole and very quickly you'll get the rat shooting out and you can kill them.

Anyway it was because of this purchase of a day's ferreting from Robinson's that I found myself one cold February morning on a Hampshire chalk down, with a long rabbit burrow that ran right the way across the down. There were about ten of us or more and certainly a dozen ferrets and the first job was to net all the holes along the line of the down, which must have stretched for a quarter of a mile, and then to position somebody at each of the holes. Then the ferrets were put in. It's fascinating to watch them. They go down, find nothing in the hole and come up again, or they might just come up, have a look and then go back down and eventually you hear the thumping of the rabbits underground; you can feel the sound vibrating through the ground you're sitting on. Soon the rabbits come shooting out into the nets and are knocked on the head, the urine is squeezed out of them and then they're hung up on a portable rack to await removal. The ferreting season comes to an end when the rabbits start breeding, around the end of February, not only because does in milk don't make very good eating but also because a rabbit won't bolt when it's pregnant, it will just stay close underground and the ferret will probably kill it and all sorts of difficulties arise with that.

On this particular day there were lots of rabbits and we came away with a rack of about thirty rabbits, perhaps four hours' work. We had been enlivened with very good bacon and sausage sandwiches and good strong tea before we set out and although the morning was cold, we were well wrapped up and it was dry and bright and we had the most magic day. The great thing about any occupation of this type and certainly any field sport is that because you have to be focused on what you're doing, it takes your mind off your worries. I always remember an old farmer, wearing an old coat of his grandfather's and on a horse with a harness tied together with string, lolloping along on a Northumbrian hill and saying, 'You canna be vexed on a day like this.' And that's rather what that day ferreting was like; you couldn't be vexed, we took our rabbits which we knew were going to be sold for consumption and went to the pub for a drink and then went home, at peace with the world.

As a total non sequitur, a friend of mine who was planning a ball said to her young helpers, 'We'll have a Ferris wheel,' and they looked at her and said, 'Surely ferrets can't turn a wheel that people can sit on!' So nice to know that young people know about ferrets even if they don't know about Ferris wheels.

The Sportsman's Day is always particularly poignant for me because it was here a few years ago that I heard of the death of my friend, Maggie. I didn't mention Maggie in *Spilling the Beans* because when I was writing it she was not long dead and it was too painful. She was, I suppose, my best friend in Scotland. I first met her at an AA meeting which she attended with her old dog, Sybil, a Labrador who loved meetings. Sybil used to come into the room, greet everybody and then lie down by Maggie's chair and when we all stood up to say the serenity prayer, Sybil would stand up and bark and join in with us. Maggie became my sponsee and then my very dear friend. She was a Borderer born and bred and was proud of her background, proud of her three children, even prouder, if anything, of her grandchildren and she was, I suppose, the most egalitarian person I ever met. She used to say we're all Jock Tamson's bairns, Jock Tamson being God. Many times I'd be going to the cinema or somewhere with her, and you'd see this group of rough boys kicking a ball about or something, the sort of behaviour to make middle-aged women nervous, and they'd all come rushing up and say, 'Halloo, halloo, Maggie!' She knew them all, she knew their parents, and she was just enormous fun.

I remember standing outside a restaurant next to the cinema at Fort Kinnaird where we were going to see some film; there was music coming out as we were hanging around waiting for the doors to open and soon there we were bopping about like a couple of mad old things. And we used to go racing together down to Kelso. She was a great racing woman who knew a lot about horses and she would ring me up and I would put on the bets; I suppose in any given year we would probably bet about £1,000. She had cousins who trained horses in Yorkshire and she would ring up to see where their horses were running and whether they were expected to do well. But more especially she was the friend I went hunting with; car following.

I would cook some beef and make what Maggie described as the best beef sandwiches in the world and she would make spinach soup, which, given the varying condition of her Thermos flasks would either end up in us or on the floor of my car – we took my car because she didn't like getting her cars dirty – but it was very good soup when we got to eat it. We would set off bright and early and she knew where all the remotest meets were and all the short cuts and we would go down and follow the Berwickshire, of which we were both friends, and just have a lovely day out. We would go to hunt functions and she knew everyone and introduced me to the great doyennes of East Lothian: Beatrice Broon-Lindsay from Coulston and Lady Mariath Hay, formerly of Yester House in Gifford, a beautiful seventeenth-century mansion with interiors designed by William Adam and, following his death, his son Robert.

Maggie had problems accepting AA in the beginning because she said that if she didn't drink her friends would find her boring and dull. This is a feature not uncommon in people in early recovery. However she got terribly ill and she said to me, 'Do you know, darling, that Beatrice Broon-Lindsay said that the only place to be was around Maggie Burns's bed and I really couldn't have been more boring and dull so they must love me for myself.' That was the breakthrough she needed and she never looked back. When she got cancer, her family, who live in different parts of the world, arranged that they and all their children should come home for what would be Maggie's last Christmas. I would do the cooking. It was going to be a rather sad occasion, until the week before Christmas she got the all-clear, she'd responded well to the chemotherapy and the cancer had gone, so you can imagine what a happy Christmas it was; Maggie just sat there grinning from ear to ear the entire time. But sadly the cancer returned and she said to me, 'You know I don't think I'm going to beat it this time.' And she didn't.

I was at the Sportsman's Day when her daughter rang me to tell me she had finally gone. When I was a child I learned to count by counting out change from the collection tins for the Imperial Cancer Research Fund of which my father was treasurer. He had lost his beloved goddaughter to cancer at a very early age and was driven to speak and to collect an enormous amount of money for cancer research, somewhere around £8 million in the late 1950s and early 1960s. That was more than fifty years ago and still we haven't beaten this hideous illness. It is one to which I have lost so many friends and to which so many people have lost friends and relatives and no doubt many more will do so. It isn't something that I anticipate getting because there's never been a single incident of it in my family and I'm a great believer in genetic strains of illness. God knows what I will die of because my family either died of the drink, which isn't likely to cause me any problems nowadays, please God, or in the case of my mother and my brother of a heart condition that I don't have.

Maggie's death took a lot of enjoyment out of my life in Scotland. It was also a great loss to Scotland, much the poorer without her continual battles to keep open hospitals in East Lothian and other weighty matters. Poor Gordon Brewer, who presents *Newsnight Scotland*, was forever being nagged by her. Her illness gave me an opportunity to see quite how insane the National Health Service is. Maggie died in the new Royal Infirmary, a hospital on which they spent a fortune of taxpayers' money and then proceeded to bring up the food from Wales in refrigerated chiller vans. There are no kitchens as such. Everything, even the toast, is brought up and heated in some form of microwave or combination oven. The end result, I have to tell you, was quite disgusting. Yet when people are in hospital, they need the best food they can get and they certainly aren't getting it at the new Royal Infirmary. I feel quite strongly too that it's an insult to my adopted country that they cannot provide their own food for their own people and buy it in from Wales. We know that the National Health Service is haemorrhaging money and looking at ways to cut back on expenditure and is saying that it's now adopting a new, greener approach and discouraging patients from eating meat as a result. Whatever patients eat is as nothing compared to the food miles and carbon emissions acquired in transporting food something like 300 miles for every meal. Those in government seem to have lost all common sense and of course the autumn showed how much it was missing in the whole economy, in banking, and in all forms of production. Each era in history has its own stamp and the one for the first part of the twenty-first century surely has to be greed.

I have never owned a property and I don't suppose I ever will so I've never applied for a mortgage. I don't think I have any credit ratings in any event. But one hears about the whole business of the investment in the sub-prime market, where mortgages were offered to people in trailer parks that they simply couldn't afford, just so that the bankers could stack up the numbers and get their bonuses. I was at breakfast in the dining room at the Goring Hotel right at the beginning of the whole sub-prime scandal and there were some bankers sitting at the next table. When finally there was just one left I said to him, 'Why did you all do this?' He said, 'Well, everybody's entitled to have a roof over their head.' And I said, 'Yes, but they're not entitled to own it if they can't afford it, and don't tell me that's what it was about anyway. I don't think compassion and banking go hand in hand.'

That foul man, Gordon Brown, makes me so angry, and that's an opinion I'm quite prepared to justify to anyone who wants the argument. Do we remember no more boom and bust? Do we remember that unctuous, prudent Chancellor? Which side of our faces are we laughing on now? He's the man who sold our gold reserves for $200 an ounce, reserves that are now worth $900 for the same ounce and left us naked and unprotected against a recession. The man who allowed the Treasury to advise councils and charities alike to invest in Iceland which was offering 7 per cent, when a small child could have worked out that the GDP of Iceland could never have borne that extreme level. I had an ex-brother-in-law who once went to prison for doing what Iceland in effect did. I fail to see why the Treasury and indeed everybody else couldn't see it coming. Consequently councils have lost millions. What they were doing holding millions in the first place instead of spending it to the benefit of the council taxpayer is quite beyond me, but the fact remains that they've lost millions, as have charities and all because Mr Brown's Treasury advised that they should do so. You can't really blame Alistair Darling too much; he's never been anything more than a puppet as far as I can see, struggling to rectify the mistakes that Brown made when he was Chancellor.

And now we have the crash of the banks and these massive bail-outs to rescue them which I don't understand. I thought in a capitalist society values rose and fell in line with the economy, yet the amount of money being paid by the government to save the banks would have provided £400,000 in every taxpayer's pocket. When I've been a director of companies over the years, I've always understood that I've had a certain fiscal liability for my actions, but not if you're a banker, it seems. Not only are you not expected to contribute anything to the huge pool of debts, but you're also allowed to go on drawing your bonuses as well. Fred Goodwin, the chief executive of the Royal Bank of Scotland, even succeeded in drawing his massive pension. I was a lawyer long enough to know that the first questions anybody asks are, 'Are there any discretionary clauses? Are there any let-out clauses? How binding is the contract?' And it seems that the contract wasn't binding but it sure as hell is now. It would seem that Goodwin, friend of Mr Brown – forgive the pun – has got away scot-free.

Then we have the horrendous story of Mr Brown talking to the head of Lloyds TSB at a cocktail party. It was a healthy little bank really, not one that was heading for this disaster. It had been that rare thing, prudent, until the Prime Minister, our unelected Prime Minister, talks it into taking over HBOS with all its toxic debt. I don't know how long it's going to take this world of ours to recover from these disasters. The only benefit I can possibly see arising from it is that we may come to be reliant on our own food, and stop importing all this horrid, cheap, tacky food for the supermarkets to sell to us. Little wonder then that the populace gets ill. Although personally I'm not affected, it makes me very angry indeed.

On a lighter note, September is the month when my new books are published. This year's was *Clarissa's Comfort Food* which was the book, as I mentioned earlier, that I had such problems with my computer over. Eventually it got to bed and I believe has done very well. It's published by Kyle Cathie whom I have known for many years, ever since I went to Books for Cooks in 1987 and she, having been very senior in established publishing houses, started her own publishing house that has gone from strength to strength.

Kyle also published, at her diktat I have to say, rather than mine, *A Greener Life*, which Johnny Scott and I wrote, covering everything you would ever want to know about growing your own vegetables, keeping your livestock, and self-sufficiency in general, down to making soap from bracken or making paints from washes made from natural materials. Curiously, it is a book that has sold particularly well in London and urban areas. I suppose it's a wish-fulfilment book for a great many people while those who are actually doing it probably know what they're doing anyway. Johnny's sections of the book are noted for their rather robust comments. In the section he wrote on dealing with various types of vermin, when it comes to foxes, he says, 'Phone the kennels.' And of course you can't do that any more now. But if you have problems with urban foxes, buy lots of white pepper and scatter it all around the place because the foxes don't like it and go somewhere else. White pepper also works on cats and mice.

In order to promote a newly published book, the author has to do the rounds and one of my delights in such instances is appearing on the *Alan Titchmarsh Show*. On this occasion we cooked the chocolate Bakewell tart which was rather more successful than my previous appearance on the show when we were supposed to be, against my better judgement, cooking crebines, boned pig's trotters, and the food stylist had left out the one step in the recipe that you actually couldn't work around. However Alan Titchmarsh proved what a true professional he is and said, 'I've always wanted to do this . . .' and did that bit bending his knees pretending to walk downstairs into a cellar to keep us amused until someone found the food stylist. I have to tell you that the chocolate tart was a delight.

My other favourite promotional programme is the *Paul O'Grady Show*. Paul is the most enchanting man, great fun and with enormous energy. The first time I appeared on his show I remember I was sitting in the make-up room when he came in and within two seconds we were discussing the various attributes of black puddings; he of course, being a Lancastrian, liked his Bury black pudding whereas I was saying that the best black pudding in the country was made by Stuart Higginson in Grange-over-Sands in Cumbria.

For this appearance it was proposed that we should make pastry and so there was Paul and myself and Will Young, the chap who won *Pop Idol*, all lined up in a row with our various bowls of flour and water and butter, ready to make pastry. They were surprised to discover that it was not quite as easy as you think it is. I expect this was largely because there wasn't a food stylist on the show so the amounts had been measured out in a rather cavalier fashion, and also of course the art of pastry is to have everything cold but the arc-lights had heated the ingredients up a treat so that there was a lot of very sticky pastry around attached to everybody's hands. So I gave the charming young singer a ball I had made earlier, for him to roll out and he was terribly overexcited to be rolling out pastry properly.

Another time when I was on Paul's show he had a flea circus and there was a small boy helping with it who was absolutely riveted (he often has quite young children helping him on the show). I didn't tell him that I was every bit as riveted as he was because I had always believed that flea circuses actually involved fleas rather than an incredibly clever piece of confidence trickery.

Partridge and Potato Cutlets

This is a dish which my grandmother's chef, Fuzduh, used to make with chicken, but it is equally good with partridge. It's a dish to make if you have mashed potato or baked potatoes left over or if you have some extra cooked partridge. In fact, there are so many partridge around these days and they are quite cheap so when you are roasting some partridge just roast a few more so that you can strip the meat off them and use it for this dish.

4 baked potatoes
1 egg
salt and freshly ground black pepper
1 onion
3 tablespoons oil
12oz (350g) partridge meat
½ teaspoon ground ginger
1 teaspoon garam masala
1 teaspoon turmeric
1 large tomato
3 tablespoons flat-leafed parsley, finely chopped
a bowl of fine breadcrumbs or matzah meal

If your potatoes are cold, heat them slightly with a little olive oil but they must be dry for this dish. Scoop out the flesh and work in the egg, lightly beaten, and the salt and pepper until you have a soft dough. Chop your onion and fry in the oil until golden. Peel, deseed and chop the tomato. Fry with the onion at the end of its cooking time. Add the partridge meat which you have cut into smallish pieces and stir until it is heated through. Season with salt and pepper, add the spices and a little water. Simmer until the water is absorbed and evaporated and then stir in the chopped parsley. Divide the potato into patties and flatten out each patty and put a spoonful of the partridge mixture into the middle of it and close it up so that the meat is entirely contained within the potato. Roll the patties in the breadcrumbs and then shallow fry them in hot oil, drain off in kitchen paper and serve hot.

October

A stitch in time, saves nine

October, in my view, is the month of anticipation. It's coming up to the season of hunting proper, of shooting pheasants, of coursing, in the days when we had it, of pony trials, and now of course what used to be known as cubbing or autumn hunting has merely been transformed into puppy training, where you get a lot of very young hounds trying to trace a laid scent which it isn't in their blood to do.

It's the month to get ready your winter stores, make sure your wood pile is full and your coal sacks are in and it's also the month to prepare your tappen. I was very tempted to set a prize for the first person to tell me what a tappen was but then I thought that might prove too complicated. A tappen is the plug made of leaves and resin and fat which a grizzly bear prepares and inserts into its rectum to make sure that during its period of hibernation no insects intrude and lay their eggs which might cause disease in the sleeping grizzly. I do think this is the most clever thing. One doesn't think of bears as being terribly intelligent but I must say that is amazing. I watched an extremely interesting documentary on polar bears and grizzly bears and was fascinated to discover that the polar bear is in fact a grizzly bear that adapted itself after the ice age froze the Arctic Circle so that it could live on the ice and catch seals and fish and became completely carnivorous. Yet another example that climate change is cyclical, albeit over many centuries. It would be interesting to see if the polar bear, which is now having problems because it can't swim the distances it needs to get from the polar ice to the mainland and back again, will re-adapt.

The first weekend in October sees the Melton Mowbray Food Festival which has been going for five years and was the brainchild of one of my most unlikely heroes, Matthew O'Callaghan, the vegetarian Labour councillor for the town of Melton Mowbray. The first two festivals were held in the cattle market in Melton, which gave them a totally different feel to all the other food fairs you find around the country, and were absolutely brilliant. In the first year, Matthew went out and looked at the diversity of the East Midlands and so there was a large West Indian stand with a West Indian steel band where they were cooking such dishes as jerk chicken and goat curry on coal pots. There were also a number of Indian stands with some really delicious food because there are large Indian and Pakistani settlements in Leicester and other parts of the West Midlands. Also in the mix were people like Jan McCourt from Northfield Farm selling his excellent meat, a bison producer, fen farm venison and Mrs Botterill who raises the most wonderful geese and Barbary ducks. That first year was, I think, the best food festival I've ever been to. I was particularly happy on that occasion because on a very good bookseller's stand I found a copy of Hannah Glasse's book on confectionery which in all my years as a bookseller I had never actually seen. The great thing with these fairs is to get in early and set up your stand and then you can wander around and see what everybody else is doing and what sort of delicious products there are on offer.

The second year the food festival was once again in the market and they had a very interesting section on food history where for the first time I ate the strange early English fruit called the chequer which I think is from the same family as the medlar, which is what people used to chew instead of chewing gum to keep away hunger pangs in the Middle Ages. James Martin, the television chef, was one of the people giving demonstrations and for some reason best known to himself, as he's a large, fit, Yorkshire man, demanded that he be given a bodyguard. I don't know what he imagined was going to happen to him to need a bodyguard of six men to escort him at all times. Maybe he thought the women would try to tear his clothes off. Anyway, there was me, number three on the Animal Liberation Front death list, sitting happily at my table with nobody but Isabel, my assistant, and my penknife to defend me. So when it was my turn to give a demonstration, I came across a group of pike-men and musketeers in costume with a fife player and a drum who had been part of the history exhibition and I said to them, 'Come on, lads, you're my bodyguards!' And so we marched into the food area and I said, 'See, I too can have a bodyguard!' It brought the roof down; everybody was cheering and laughing and whistling. Unfortunately James Martin was still backstage and I don't think he's speaking to me.

Regrettably, as is so often the case, the funding authority then cut back on their grant and the festival was forced to move to Brooksby Melton Agricultural College which is some miles outside Melton on the Leicester road and not that easy to find even with all the signage in the world. While it is still a good food festival, it has become less unusual and appealing. And of course there were the normal problems with people cooking at the festival because either they cooked outside and it being October there was a strong risk of the customers getting wet while they queued up for their burgers and sausages or whatever, or they cooked inside in which case there was an awful lot of smoke. It's quite interesting that at this particular food festival they don't have crappy white vans selling compressed meat pulp as they do at so many fairs. All the food options on offer are for really good products. The difference in taste between a hamburger made out of properly reared meat and one from a white van is so enormous, you would scarcely believe it. The Northfield Farm van has a quote from me on it which says, 'Quite the best burgers I've ever eaten.'

One of the delights of this Melton Mowbray Food Festival was meeting Anjum Anand who has a television series called *Indian Food Made Easy* and is to my mind quite the best of the television cooks of recent years. When I watch her programmes I actually want to eat the food. Her stand was next door to mine so I had an opportunity to talk to her at some length. I went and tasted some of her food backstage because thanks to Health and Safety you're not allowed to give food out to the customers to eat, although I have to say it doesn't stop me. And it was delicious, absolutely yummy. She has written two books, one to go with each series, and I can only suggest that you go out and buy them because her food is very different from what Indian restaurants in this country serve and has fresh flavours and original ideas.

We mused over the notion, as one does on these sorts of occasions, of doing a joint programme in India, where she showed me India and I talked about the influences of the Raj, and we had a splendid time. Unfortunately I'm quite certain nothing will ever come of it but it is a project that I would really like to do and there aren't many of those left these days, I can tell you.

After staying for a couple of days with Jan, to recuperate from the festival, I finally drove home again loaded with good things to put in my freezer. I haven't written much about Alcoholics Anonymous in this book, although not because I'm not still going to meetings. In fact during these rather hideous thirteen months of unending travel, the only stability and consistency in my life were the AA meetings that I attended around the country, my *Where to Find* in both London and the rest of the country firmly in the glove compartment of my car. The great thing about walking into a strange AA meeting is that you feel instantly at home; not only are you welcomed by the people there but you know that they will understand what you are saying, however strange it may seem. One of the nicest surprises was when I was going to a meeting in London and walking down a long alley to get to it and I saw the shape (because by this time my eyes were deteriorating quite fast) of a young man waving and jumping about at the end of the alley. When I got there, I was delighted to find that he was the greeter for the meeting, his mother being a great friend of mine. The last time I'd seen him I was quite convinced that he would be dead before I saw him again because he was, although young, in such a bad state and gave no sign of giving up alcohol. And there he was, looking incredibly well and with several months of sobriety under his belt. We gave each other a huge hug and sat next to each other in the meeting.

One of the good things about AA these days is the number of young people who are coming in. Partly because they started their drinking careers at a much earlier age than my generation did but also I suppose partly because people know more about AA now and so are prepared to give it a try early and even if it doesn't take the first time, with any luck they'll come back a bit later on.

One of the stories I love about AA in England is that it was started by two men over here in 1947, having originated in America in 1934. One of the two men was an extremely rich master of foxhounds who'd had a very good war and had come back to an enabling wife, an enabling butler, who both covered up for him, and an endless supply of money. It would seem that there was nothing that would make him hit rock bottom and think that his life was so bad that he had to get into recovery until he woke up one morning and couldn't remember the names of his hounds. He found this such a dreadful prospect and the worst possible thing that could happen to him that he rushed off to America to find out about AA and he and an Irish peer brought it back. The first meeting they had, and there's a plaque on the wall to prove it, was in the ballroom of the Dorchester Hotel in May 1947, just in time for me to be born, says she smugly, and the only newspaper that would publish an advertisement for it, with or without money, was the *Financial Times*.

One hears wonderful stories of the early characters in AA. There was a man called Ironing Board Arthur who was too afraid to speak or to say anything about himself and one of the few women in AA said to him, 'Why don't you speak, Arthur?' He said he wouldn't know what to say. And she said, 'Well, just talk about what you know about, anything, just to open your mouth.' During his last stay in a mental institution he had been taught how to make an ironing board and so he launched into an account of how to make one and went on for forty minutes. Nobody stopped him. After that he started to get better, though he used to tell amazing stories of his experiences on the twelve-step list; bear in mind that there weren't so many members then and twelve-steppers, if you ring up and ask for help, are the people who are sent out to take you to a meeting. Anyway Arthur used to go and answer the calls and physically take people to meetings. On one occasion he was told to meet somebody outside South Ken tube station and so he rushed up to a man and said, 'Right – I've come to take you to the meeting!' The man said, 'I don't know what you're talking about.' But Arthur threw him into the back of his van and said, 'Don't argue with me.' The man was protesting, 'But I'm a petty officer!' And Arthur was insisting, 'Well, that makes no difference, we have peers of the realm.' So he took him off to the meeting and let him out of the van, spluttering and coughing and swearing, and it turned out that he wasn't an alcoholic at all and had been standing there waiting for his wife. I'm happy to say that life is rather more ordered nowadays.

I had to drive home after the Melton Mowbray event during the hours of daylight because my cataracts made driving at night quite a frightening experience and I couldn't really see where I was going. I only had a couple of weeks at home this time. That's the trouble with my life, I get home and settle, relax and really enjoy it and then I have to go off again. This time I was going to see my London doctor, Michael Gormley, about my cataracts. He is one of three brothers, one of whom is the sculptor who made the Angel of the North and those wonderful figures that look out into the Irish Sea at Crosby beach, near Liverpool, and are submerged when the tide comes in and then revealed when it goes out again. The third brother is the chap who is head of the Disaster Emergency Committee who you frequently see on television, talking about fundraising for the latest disaster. Anyway, Michael recommended me to an ophthalmic surgeon by the name of Mr Jonathan Jagger, whose consulting rooms were curiously in the back of the London

Clinic, which was very strange for me in a way because that's where I was born.

Mr Jagger was the most delightful man and made my consultation very easy because when talking to me about what would happen and the nature of the eye, he put it into food terms. So he said, when you're born your eye is like pure water and over the years it thickens and becomes the consistency of very expensive hot chocolate and the preliminary stages of the operation would return it to somewhere around the level of a good milk-shake. When my grandmother had her cataracts done, in those days you had to lie in bed for a week with sandbags on either side of your head, so she said, 'Well, you might as well do my bunions too if I've got to lie down for a week.' Nowadays the operation actually takes about twenty minutes. I suppose you're there for half a day having the eye-drops put in to dilate the pupil and then they hoover out the lens with its attached cataracts and insert an artificial lens. I apparently have very small pupils which is why the cataracts had come on so quickly. I've always had a horror of anything being done to my eyes so I was really quite apprehensive about the whole thing but Mr Jagger couldn't have been more charming. We made a date for the beginning of November but before then I had my appointment to keep in the West Country.

I had promised Alison Hawes, who you may remember is the Countryside Alliance rep for the West Country who was so helpful to me earlier in the year, that I would go and do an event for her and she had asked if I would speak to the Four Burrow Hunt. The rather curious name of this hunt is because at either end of its territory are rather large rabbit burrows which were presumably commercial warrens originally. I spent a night in Hampshire and trucked on to the West Country. I spend so much of my life travelling around the country that I am constantly appalled at the state of the hotels, the poor quality of the staff, the lack of comfort and the low standards of the food. It's not surprising that we don't have the tourist industry we should have or that people don't go on holiday in this country because really it takes as much effort to cook good food as it does to cook bad food and yet time and again you get this lack of care, this lack of consideration, so when you do find a hotel that is worth it, do treasure it.

I arrived in Redruth at teatime and decided to have a nap before the excitements of the evening. But my bedroom was so cold that I, who can sleep anywhere and at any time, couldn't manage to get to sleep because I was shivering so much, even after I had piled every piece of towelling and whatever you could think of on top of me. I managed to warm up in time to get some sleep but no effort had been made to turn on any heating. As is always the case with hunting events, the evening itself was a delight. The company is always good, the craic is good and one feels really welcomed.

The next day I left the Four Burrow and went to stay with my friend Annie Mallalieu for a night. I was really looking forward to seeing her. The only trouble was that I was heading along the A30 when a lorry turned over and shed its load and we were all diverted. This did lead to difficulties because my eyes were now so bad that I couldn't actually read the map properly and so by the time I'd managed to get to her house it was teatime. So I missed spending the best part of the day with her, but we had a very jolly evening and a lot of people came over from the Exmoor Staghounds. Stag hunting is another one of those sports that people are given misconceptions about, usually by the antis.

In fact I knew nothing about it myself until the *Clarissa and the Countryman* years when Johnny Scott and I went down to sign books in Devon and to have a day out with the staghounds. I went with Tim Yandall, the chairman, in his old Volvo while Johnny was on a horse and I couldn't have had a better guide. He explained to me what was happening and how it worked. It is the oldest of mounted hunting with hounds and there are various periods in the year when you hunt the stags and when you hunt the hinds and when you can hunt both. This culling of the runts and the older beasts is necessary in order to keep the stock strong. The deer, whether stag or hind, is chosen to be cut out of the woodland where it's living and killed. It is very difficult to cut out an animal from dense woodland which is where they live in that part of the world, in the deep coombs, and so they send in older, more mature hounds called tufters, who cut out the deer and drive it into the open where the scent is then pursued by younger hounds with the mounted field following, until the stag is brought to bay. Not, as you are constantly told, in a state of exhaustion and nearly driven to death. Stags turn and stand at bay when they think they've had enough; their first instinct is to run and then they will turn and stand. At that point the man with a gun goes in and kills the stag so that it is not torn down by hounds or torn to pieces or any of the emotive terms that the antis use in such circumstances.

Deer are a form of vermin. If you have the suitable amount of deer they won't destroy too much in the countryside and will then be tolerated. I am talking here about the red deer, the largest of the English native deer, hunted as a source of food for centuries. The King's deer were sacred to the King and those he allowed to hunt them, and the penalties for taking deer if you were not so licensed were very severe indeed, including incarceration, mutilation and even death. One of the most illegal actions of Robin Hood was to take the King's deer. If you lived in a deer forest, you were not allowed to have a dog large enough to take deer unless its middle toe was removed which meant that it couldn't run fast enough to take a deer.

A curious survey conducted in the Second World War showed that people whose families have historically lived in the environs of deer forests will not eat venison. During the war there was quite a lot of venison available, largely because the American troops on Exmoor and Dartmoor used to take their machine-gun practice by shooting herds of deer, but when the meat went into the butchers in those areas, people simply wouldn't buy it. In the race memory was strongly imposed the fact that it was an illegal offence that could result in very nasty penalties indeed.

Red deer stags can be extremely dangerous animals, especially during the rut or breeding season. The roar of the male stag at this time of the year is an intimidating enough sound. A friend of mine was once riding her bicycle in a mist through Richmond Park and suddenly on either side of her she heard two stags bellowing at each other and saw the tips of their antlers through the mist. She realised she was right between the two, and if they decided to clash there wouldn't be a lot left of her. But even in more ordinary circumstances it's best to avoid them during the rut. Stay home and watch it on television. I have been fortunate enough to watch two stags clashing. It's an impressive sight, powerful and testosterone-fuelled, and very often what happens is that while these big beasts are fighting over a herd of hinds, the little runt of the litter nips in and covers them all, so that a lot of theories about survival of the fittest and breeding of the most perfect are not always true.

When we were making *Clarissa and the Countryman*, we went up to the Isle of Mull to film the hind cull, which is when you take out a hind if it's old, bloody, yelled or damned. In other words if it's too old to survive the winter, or it's got a bloodied wound, or yelled is barren, and damned means a hind that for one reason or another, like loss of teeth or illness or broken bones, will simply not survive the winter. The alternative is to allow the deer to starve to death and even the most rabid antis might perhaps admit that this isn't a very good idea. It's worth remembering that when stalking or indeed undertaking any country pursuit you need to meld as much as possible into the background so that if you keep still you are not obviously visible. I was slightly surprised that people don't register why you want to wear the sort of clothes that you do. I suppose that walkers wear bright and obvious garments so that when they fall and the poor mountain rescue team have to go and rescue them they can be easily seen, but this is not the case for country people. On this occasion Johnny managed to shoot a hind and Esme, our director at the time and a vegetarian, even insisted on filming the gralloch which is where you get rid of the umbles or the guts of the deer, hence the term 'eating umble pie', which are the bits that were left for the huntsmen.

Venison is a most delicious meat. You don't of course want to kill a stag in the rut and eat that because the level of adrenalin and testosterone that pours off the meat is quite apparent to the human nose from a long way away, but all other forms of deer are tasty. And yet we export most of it. During the foot and mouth outbreak when we couldn't export venison, people started to eat it, restaurants put it on their menus because it was cheap and people came in and said, 'Gosh, we really like this!' They came into my bookshop and asked, 'Have you got a book that tells me how to cook it?' And I didn't so I wrote one which is really the reasoning behind *The Game Cookbook*, arguably the best of all my recipe books, which I wrote with Johnny Scott. People are afraid of cooking venison and quite rightly because it's very easy to ruin. Here are one or two points to bear in mind: venison, like squid, should be cooked very fast or very slow and because it's a lean meat with no fat you need either to bard it with fat or marinate it in some way. You have to be careful how it's butchered as if you leave the silver skins on (if you've eaten venison you will know what I'm talking about), they will contort the venison while it's cooking because they will shrink and make it tough. And here's a useful piece of information from my friend Claire Macdonald, cookery writer and co-owner of the famed Kinloch Lodge on Skye, which is that beetroot contains an enzyme that when cooked with venison will tenderise even the toughest beast.

Walnut biscuits

I love biscuits made with walnut. I find them chewier and more flavoursome than the almond variety and just as easy to make.

4 egg whites
4oz (110g) pulverised walnuts
2oz (50g) chopped walnuts
4oz (110g) soft brown sugar
2 teaspoons plain flour

Preheat the oven to 150°C/300°F/ gas mark 2. Whisk the egg whites stiffly and fold in the other ingredients. Arrange sheets of baking paper on baking trays and put dollops of the mixture on to it. They will not run as much as almond biscuits and so can be fairly close together. Bake for about 20 minutes, until lightly brown and firm. Remove them from the baking sheet and cool on a wire rack, and store in an airtight tin as they will go sticky otherwise.

November

A-hunting we will go
Hey ho, tally ho, a-hunting we will go

November is a good time to go to Borough Market. Nearly ten years ago, Jennifer and I opened the first Borough Market, which had been put together by Peter Gott of Sillfield Farm in Cumbria, producer of the finest pork and wild boar, Randolph Hodgson of Neal's Yard Dairy in London, and the food writer Henrietta Green and counted among its number about ten core suppliers, including Jan McCourt of Northfield Farm and West Country Park Venison. It was a small market and one that as Jennifer and I milked the goat to declare the market open – literally – we did not think would survive more than two or three years. It was making use of a space under the railway arches at London Bridge. Now all these years on, the market is a thriving, buzzing place with a great many suppliers and brings a lot of much needed resources to the area.

The market was originally founded in the Middle Ages. I believe, because I've not yet managed to see the original trust document, that it was founded to supply fresh food to the population of Southwark which in medieval times was the red light district of London, where all the brothels and bathhouses and theatres and all things disreputable found their home over the years. The market went through many changes and by the time the produce market was opened was mainly a supplier of wholesale fruit and vegetables. In my clubbing days I ran a club on Hay's Wharf where the main customers at lunchtime were the wholesalers from the market who came to eat their dinner and go home to bed because they kept very early hours.

The current produce market is open on Thursday afternoon in a limited fashion and then on Friday and Saturday, Saturday being the day when the young and fashionable who live south of the river haul themselves out of bed at midday and decide to go to Borough to eat, so it's very crowded with people eating the delicious food on offer rather than actually buying produce. Outside the Christmas season, the footfall is, I think, about 55,000 a week and the trustees of the market earn somewhere in the region of £250,000 a month. It is the most perfect London market, in my view, in that you have country producers side by side with people selling very expensive Chinese and Japanese teas, home-made bakery goods, the most delicious chocolate brownies and men in kaffiyehs selling olives and pickled lemons and all the goodies of the Middle East. Borough Market is not, of course, a farmers' market because under the Farmers' Markets Association rules producers have to be within a twenty-mile radius of markets throughout the country, extended to forty miles for London markets. But at Borough you have producers coming from Cumbria, from the West Country, from all sorts of places not necessarily even in Britain. London has always been full of foreign traders so that the importers merely represent that cosmopolitan, melting pot side of the capital city.

My favourite stands are Furness Fish and Game with lovely Les Salisbury bringing the produce of Cumbria to London where in season you will see game hanging in fur and feather. When we were filming the programme on Hannah Glasse we got a hare from them but it was actually cleaned on a table in front of Peter Gott's Sillfield Farm stand which is, besides

Northfield, really the only place to go and buy pork goods at the market: bacon and haslet and hams and brawn and all those delicious cuts that are so hard to find in this day and age. There is a real buzz that the best place to go for breakfast is Maria's little café which has now been moved into the middle of the market where they make – and I say this emphatically – the best bubble and squeak you will ever eat.

Brindisa, who import all that is best from Spain, have a restaurant there where you can have excellent tapas and very good coffee and, if you're drinking, the best Spanish wines and sherries and suchlike. And Neal's Yard cheese emporium is located under the arches rather than on a stand, where you can buy delicious English cheeses. In fact, there are stalls selling almost everything you can think of in the food line. There's even a man who comes up from the West Country and sells and cooks hand-dived scallops. You would think, therefore, wouldn't you, that with this thriving market that arose out of nothing in what was just a non-productive site, that the trustees of the market would be happy, would collect their money, and encourage the market's development, but again there is something rotten in the state of Denmark because (that's a quote from *Hamlet*, it has nothing to do with Denmark) they are trying to put up the rents. Not for the wholesalers, who are protected by all sorts of conditions under the original charter, I believe, but for the produce market traders. Compare that to the iconic Boccaria market in Barcelona or the wonderful market in Bologna, where the traders buy their sites for very little money and in fact are subsidised by the Spanish and Italian governments to display and sell and be a resource not only for the local people but also an attraction for visitors and tourists.

The Borough Market traders went for an away day with the Boccaria and all came back absolutely gobsmacked, not just at the size and extent of the market but also at the excellent conditions and assistance they received. The same cannot be said of Borough where the traders struggle under draconian rules as to what they can and cannot do, to say nothing of our lovely Health and Safety. When I'm visiting a friend of mine who lives in Fuengirola, we go to the market and we see a pile of goat's heads at the side of a stall for people to buy, presumably to take home for their animals, but if you tried to do something like that here, you simply wouldn't be allowed to get away with it.

I remember when Peter Gott brought down a wild boar he had shot, and hung it in its pelt outside his stand and of course was not allowed to sell said wild boar because Health and Safety objected. I should add that he had shot it because it had escaped. Wild boar had died out in this country when the Victorians drew up the game laws and so do not count as game for shooting and eating, and have to be taken, kicking and screaming if you like, to the abattoir. If I was an abattoir attendant I wouldn't like to have to kill a wild boar since they are very dangerous creatures indeed.

Unsurprisingly, I suppose, ongoing battles between the market controllers and the traders, with the former trying to extract more money from the latter, have been going on throughout history. I don't know of any incidents in ancient Rome, although I'm sure there must have been some, but all through the Middle Ages the monasteries who owned the markets around the country would constantly put pressure on the traders for more money. The end result would be that another town would offer the traders a venue and so they'd go off and get a charter for a market in the other town and once it was successful the same thing would happen again. The most famous case was perhaps Shrewsbury in the twelfth century when relations got so fraught that the monks of the monastery and the traders came to blows; weapons were drawn, probably cudgels, and the sheriffs were called to bring in troops to sort out the problem. I presume the Borough Market trustees reckon that if the traders do walk, there will always be other people to fill the gap. And now that organic food production has become fashionable among the rich, I expect there will be such people but the quality will not be the same, the atmosphere will not be the same and it'll be a great pity for what is the most wonderful of institutions. It is also a rather curious fact, perhaps even a conflict of interest, in that the new chief executive officer of the market has long associations with the railways and one wonders where Network Rail stands in all this.

I discovered that historically turkeys were walked to the London markets from East Anglia, and their feet were dipped in tar in order to protect them from the road. And in fact rather than being driven to the meat market at Smithfield as one might expect they were driven to Billingsgate which was a poultry market as well as the fish market. Geese were treated in the same way. I think the meat that's being sold nowadays probably has a rather preferable manner of reaching the market.

It must have been amazing, mustn't it, watching the great flocks of geese and turkeys and the sheep and beasts that were brought from all over the country to feed London? There were farms in the Home Counties close to London that existed simply to fatten up the drovers' beasts before they were taken to Smithfield. What a noisy, messy place it must have been when live animals were still taken there. The reason why there was no butcher in St James's as I used to find to my cost when I was cooking at Wilde's Club, until Fortnum and Mason started selling fresh meat in their newly refurbished store, that is, was that Charles II couldn't bear the noise and the stink and so decreed that there was to be no butchery or abattoir in the whole area.

The opening sequence of *Clarissa and the Countryman* was Johnny and me driving sheep over London Bridge, when I was exercising my right as a freeman of the City of London to do so. The importance of being a freeman was not the driving itself, which in the old days anyone could do, but that the freeman was exempted the toll that everyone else had to pay. It must have made a huge amount of difference to the value of your flocks. That was the most extraordinary day. Johnny had brought this sheepdog bitch, Nell, down from Scotland and she had never been outside her hills in the Lammermuirs before, let alone to London and, gosh, she was a game little creature. We thought we were going to be driving nice, docile South Down sheep but instead they turned out to be black-faced mules; a mule is a cross-breed and these black-face were crossed with grey-faced Cheviots, I think, and were really very feisty sheep indeed and quite big.

When we set up the first take, they opened the pen door at the far end of London Bridge and the sheep just shot off across the bridge to the other side where fortunately there was a lorry with its ramp down waiting to take them home, blocking their exit, otherwise they'd probably have got to Smithfield on their own. So we had to bring them all back and start again, and if you look carefully at the sequence you will notice that there is quite a lot of sheep shit already on the bridge, because nobody had thought to bring a broom to sweep it off. Johnny's apprehension was not helped by that year's Master Butcher, my friend Graham Jackman, resplendent in his robes, looking over the parapet of the bridge at the Thames and saying, 'I suppose you'd say that's the largest sheep dip in Europe.' However, Nell was absolutely wonderful and we successfully crossed London Bridge with the sheep, this time slowly enough for the camera that was stationed in Fishmongers' Hall at the far end of the bridge to get some brilliant shots.

Nell, who was a very pretty dog, was a great camera-grabber. She must have been a Hollywood starlet in a previous existence, I think. She had great kohl-rimmed eyes and, rather like Tug, Johnny's terrier, whenever there was a camera running, somehow or other Nell would be in shot. But I don't think we ever really paid tribute to how wonderful Johnny's animals were during all the series, and indeed Johnny himself, who has been a sheep man for most of his farming life but it's one thing to round up sheep on your own hill, and quite another to do so on other people's land or especially on London Bridge.

Anyway, the time had now come for my first cataract operation. It was well due, after I missed the M5 turning off the M4, and I realised that perhaps I shouldn't be driving at all. It's strange the sorts of things that go through your mind when you're about to have an operation and in my case in particular an eye operation. I'm not by nature prone to negativity, you know, I tend to charge my fences head on; somebody once said of me that I threw my heart over the fence and jumped over after it which I thought was a terribly nice compliment. But I found myself unwontedly anxious and I kept thinking of all the things I had seen that mattered to me. Country things, like woodcock roading in the dusk, or I once saw a weasel dancing, and it was like a leaf blown in the wind, a large leaf, and when you looked closely, you realised it was a weasel.

Weasels dance to mesmerise their prey, especially the rabbit and it's an amazing sight of a free spirit just twirling and twisting but always with the end view in sight. There were no rabbits about, so this weasel was just either dancing for the sheer joy of it or practising. The sight of the salmon leaping up the weir at Pitlochry, driven to their spawning beds by this overwhelming desire to reproduce, and leaping amazing heights into the air, gleaming and glistening as they go. Of a fox winding its way in and out of the fence posts at a sort of slow, thoughtful pace as you heard the hounds in the distance and the hounds came, of course, because they're scent hounds, followed the fox in and out of the fence posts and by then it had gone off happily on a different track and they never found it. Of the hare turning right under the nose of a greyhound that was pursuing it at full pelt and dashing off in the other direction and by the time the greyhound had recovered the hare was lost in the woods. I thought too of all the things I've always wanted to see and that I might never see if the operation went wrong. I've never seen a woodcock carrying her young on her back, their little tiny beaks sticking up in the air. I've never seen a capercaillie in the pine forests of northern Scotland. So many things that I would like to see.

And so I went into the London Clinic. The other patients and I all sat around in our backless nighties with some rather nice dressing gowns over the top. I must say I've never quite understood the point of the backless nightie which is an extraordinarily uncomfortable garment. My mother used to remark that the food in the London Clinic was disgusting and it seems that nothing much has changed; although I only had a sandwich and a cup of tea, it's amazing how horrible a cup of tea can be. My sweet anaesthetist said, 'Oh yes, you can have a cup of tea.' So the foreign nurse, I think she was Bosnian or something like that, gave me one. After only a sip I said, 'This is quite disgusting.' The nurse said, 'Oh, our patients like our tea,' to which I replied, 'It just shows that they're considerably more polite than I am.' But she was quite taken aback when she did my tests, because as you know I'm not slim, to discover that I had immaculate blood pressure, perfect cholesterol, faultless heartbeat, excellent oxidisation or whatever it's called when you take the oxygen into the bloodstream, and she kept re-doing the tests without telling me why. Eventually I told her, 'Look, it's not the machine, you know, I actually do have all these virtues.' She said, 'And you do not have diabetes.' And I said, 'No, I do not have diabetes, I'm just fat.'

It's a curious thing, you know, being fat in this politically correct age where quite rightly you mustn't mock people for being of different nationalities or of different sexual orientations, but you're still allowed to throw mud at them for being fat. Consequently those of us who are get a lot more insults hurled at us than anybody else because the human race is given to bigotry and insult. I remained fat after I stopped drinking because the quinine in the tonic water that I drank with my gin in such quantities damaged my adrenal gland but, having said that, neither of my parents was particularly thin at the end of their lives. My father, who, I think, slept a total of four hours a day and worked incredibly hard performing surgery and seeing his patients all day and going out to raise funds by giving after-dinner speeches all night, was a large man who enjoyed his food and his drink with great gusto but nobody could have accused him of being lazy or even unfit.

Louise Leeds, the cook of my childhood, weighed the best part of twenty stone but ran an incredibly efficient kitchen with all the energy in the world. Where obesity is especially dangerous to my mind is in children, where it has been caused by eating junk foods and artificial saturated fats. When the government bangs on about fat children, they never seem to remember that it was they who sold off all the playing fields so that children have nowhere to exercise. When asked on television for my views on fat children I frequently reply that I have never seen a fat child on the hunting field so why the hell do they want to ban it?

Anyway, having survived the nurse, I was then taken off to the operating theatre where I lay down on my stretcher and received my injection. They don't give you a general anaesthetic for cataract operations any more: they give you intravenous Valium, which sort of floats you out of the world so that you're aware that something's going on but not what, and a local anaesthetic to the eye. It's amazing what an efficient operation it is these days. After my injection, off I floated and the next thing I knew, I was coming round in my cubicle with a large dressing over my eye, being offered a rather less horrible cup of tea and a not very nice ham sandwich. I was alive and was told that the operation had been a total success.

My friend Sally Merison came and took me down to Hampshire to recuperate. I spent the journey in a sort of fugue and when we got there I went straight to bed. The last thing I remember as I had a cup of Bovril before bed was Kipper sitting by the Aga, staring at me with a look of great concern on his face because my eye looked rather like an exaggerated bug. The dressing was over a sort of raised plastic frame and I did look very strange indeed. Then I went to sleep and that was that.

The next morning I woke up and I was rather like a small child at Christmas, 'Can I open it yet, can I open it yet?' At seven o'clock on a beautiful sunny morning, I went off into the bathroom and removed the patch and saw the world, no longer through what seemed like a dirty window that hasn't been washed for years, but bright and sparkling and with every blade of grass and every leaf and every bird all in the most glorious technicolour. Even Kipper, when he finally came to greet me and was greatly relieved to see that I didn't still have this bug eye, sparkled with colours that I never knew he possessed. It was quite the most extraordinary feeling. There's a tribe in the Andes who keep the children who are going to be priests in the dark or in a gloomy cave for the first four years of their life so that when they come out into the sunshine their minds are, I imagine, quite literally blown away by the bright light and colours. I felt rather like that.

What they don't tell you, although the anaesthetist had hinted at it, is how long it takes for the eye to adjust to the brain or vice versa, so that you're able to see really properly. They say not to drive for three days and I didn't and not to strain your eye, so buy magnifiers if you have difficulty reading. After the first eye operation I was fine for reading because the other eye was still as it had been and I could read with that, but it does take six weeks, on an ascending scale obviously, so that every day it got better and my brain adjusted more to the changes. But what a miracle of modern science it really is. My father used to say that the greatest achievements in modern medicine were to be found in surgery – well, he would say that, wouldn't he, because he was a surgeon – but I do think that there was an awful lot of truth in that. He used to say, 'Remember how Charles II died, he died of the worst excesses of the best doctors of the day.' They shaved his head and anointed it with boiling pigeon dung, they put the urine of young babies on the soles of his feet but he died anyway. At least they didn't force him to eat muesli. My father hated muesli. And it hasn't changed a lot, it's just in better packaging.

I can't say if my father was right in his view of the medical profession but I do know that when I was in my treatment centre there were an awful lot of people addicted to prescribed drugs which perhaps they should never have been given in the first place. The remit for Valium, for instance, when it first came out was that it should never be prescribed for more than three weeks and the third week should be on a diminishing dose to wean the patient off it. By and large the medical profession obviously didn't read that advice because they handed it out like sweeties; there are now whole towns in America committing suicide because they have reached the end of their tolerance level to Valium's modern replacement, Prozac, and it doesn't work any more so they fall into this great black hole. I shouldn't say things like that, should I, because in the *Sun*-reader mentality that afflicts this country doctors and nurses are saints. Some of them may well be, of course, but in this human race of ours you don't expect 100 per cent sainthood and so you must allow me my cynicism.

So the surgery was a great success and I hope you'll be pleased to hear that I have now had the second one done and that was equally successful. It means I may not have to peer at you quite so strangely if I see you at a game fair or at a country show somewhere. It does present a problem, however, if I've met you in the last few years, because I may not recognise you, not having ever seen you properly. I had the second cataract done in the King Edward VII Hospital for Officers and Gentlemen, nowadays the Sister Agnes, after the woman who founded it, and I must say that the actual stay in the hospital was a much nicer experience. And the food was considerably better. The sweet man who brought me my sandwich and my pot of tea in this instance (not a plastic cup) also brought me unbidden a crème brûlé because he wanted me to try it and it was actually up to the standards of the best London restaurants, if not better. You may say, why is she banging on about food, which is hardly the point of a hospital where the quality and condition of the operating theatre and surgery are more important and I would reply that the quality of the food is an indicator of overall standards. After all, if people can't be bothered to produce good food, what else can't they be bothered to do?

Anyway, whatever else, the handsome Mr Jagger restored my sight to me, immaculately, and I shall remain for ever grateful. After a week's convalescence staying with Sally, convalescence being something of a misnomer as she is a person possessed of the most enormous amount of energy and her idea of a quiet week would exhaust most people in two minutes flat. But convalescence holding Kipper's paw was a great comfort; he's a dear little dog, and must have understood that I was feeling slightly under the weather. The reason was not the operation itself, as the eye was nothing more than slightly scratchy for a little while but the intravenous Valium which I didn't take to very well. Fortunately the area where I was staying had some very good AA meetings that I have been to quite regularly over the years because any alcohol addict when exposed to drugs gets strange thoughts in their heads; not that I wanted to take the beastly stuff, but it brought back all sorts of strange memories. As it says at one point in the *Big Book* of Alcoholics Anonymous: 'I have used up my right to a chemical peace of mind.'

So finally I tootled home, able to see the road ahead of me and in time to appreciate my new kitchen. I don't own my house but I had long ago promised my landlady for various reasons that I would install a new kitchen to replace what I thought was a wonderfully scruffy and old-fashioned kitchen. When I spoke to Trevor the roofer about the restoration of the dry rot, I asked him if he could organise this. He imported an immensely glamorous Russian woman called, curiously, Larissa, so as her English is not perfect we had ridiculous conversations on the telephone. I would say, 'Hello, this is Clarissa.' And she'd reply, 'Yes, yes, Larissa.' And it would take us several minutes to work out which of us was which.

She and her Austrian husband, Michael, installed my kitchen with the help of a number of Poles and Lithuanian builders. Kit and the Widow have a delightful song that says there's not a plumber left in Poland, and Armstrong and Miller do a very good sketch where they're talking with Polish accents and then one says to the other, 'It's so boring – it's so tiring having to talk with a Polish accent and pretend to be Polish just to get any work as a plumber.' But I wonder what we ever did before they got here, and I rather wonder what we'll do now that the credit crisis is driving them all back home.

There are one or two teething pains but that will always happen if work is carried out in your absence. I'm pleased with my new kitchen, but the real heroine of the hour was Amelia who moved everything out of the cupboards and then eventually moved everything back into them for the second time in the year, having already had to deal single-handedly with the chaos that builders inevitably cause. She really is a star.

One of the consolations of my kitchen was that I was able to claim back the VAT because thanks to the success of *Spilling the Beans* I might now find myself liable for that most pernicious of taxes. It seems to me appalling that whichever government introduced VAT should have seen fit to make all those who earn more than a certain amount a year tax collectors on their behalf. When it was first imposed, I was a practising barrister and the Bar Council dictated that every barrister in chambers should register, I suppose just to make the clerk's life easier. In rather pernicious mood I filled in all eleven of my Christian names on the form, which resulted in completely glitching the computer so that I ended up with three separate VAT numbers. To my satisfaction it took them quite a long time to sort it out.

I was once again obliged to pay VAT during the *Two Fat Ladies* years, but as everything in those days went through my bookshop in Edinburgh, it wasn't something that had a great impact on me. Having registered, I will no doubt find myself in a situation where I'll fall back below the VAT limit and then will have to suffer all the complications of de-registering myself again. Unless of course Hollywood decides to make a blockbuster movie out of *Spilling the Beans*, which I think is slightly unlikely. However, my accountants look after me very well and Andrew Hamilton and the talented young people, Lucy and Ramsey, who've been sorting out my affairs are really very good news indeed.

Taxes are, of course, an evil that we have always had with us. What makes me angry is that we have no control at all over what happens to the money once it is paid to the Inland Revenue. At this particular time we find ourselves paying for unwinnable wars that kill our valiant young and bring down on our heads the perhaps unsurprising hatred of the Muslim world.

Incidentally, I heard with a certain amount of relish the other day that the Blairs, having bought one of the two pavilions of the John Soane house at Wotton Underwood, find themselves unable, due to the property's class one listing – and quite rightly so, as Wotton Underwood is a magnificent set of buildings – to make any alterations, especially ones for security purposes. I wonder how long it will be before the house is back on the market again? I suppose they have the one consolation that old Mrs Brunner, who lived there when I was cooking for Graham C. Greene, would not allow the hunt, the Vale of Aylesbury, to hunt through the property so they won't be roused from their slumbers by the sound of a horn. When I was there, driving up the drive at night was slightly spooky because the only animals left in the grounds were the excessively numerous foxes which, having eaten all the other wildlife, were trying to dig up the moles because there was nothing left for them to eat and you saw their red eyes in the darkness. However by now the foxes have probably moved away, simply because of the lack of food. Otherwise Blair might have thought they were the sights of a sniper rifle and got even more paranoid.

As a single woman with no dependants, I'm somewhat at a loss to see what benefit I get from paying taxes at all. The police did succeed in catching my burglar, but not in retrieving any of my property and as he jumped bail, the case seems not to have come back to court at all.

However, there was another happy outcome at the end of the year. Twenty-seven years ago, I was quite rightly expelled from my Inn of Court which precluded me from practising as a barrister. It was one of those ridiculous situations that arise when drunks are involved. A solicitor representing somebody I knew delivered a brief to the afternoon drinking club that I was running, which I promptly put behind the bar and forgot about, thinking he just wanted me to look at the papers. I'm not quite sure how the solicitor thought that I could have been practising from a drinking club as it was by this time quite clear that I was no longer a member of chambers. In any event, the matter came to court; I wasn't there, opposing counsel complained to the Bar Council and I was disbarred. I think the Inn had had enough of me. I was not a quiet, respectable, lace-curtain drunk and no doubt brought them a lot of grief and possibly even some disrepute. Five years after this disbarment I got sober and in early recovery, with some intention of going back to the law to earn a living, I applied to the Bar Council for reinstatement. They replied that they were quite happy about this but that I must apply to my Inn of Court. Circumstances overtook me, to say nothing of a motorbike sidecar, and I never made such application.

I don't know if you are like this, but I find that in my soul I have little stained-glass windows where the light shines through pictures of those places where I've been happy, or which are special to me, and Gray's Inn was certainly one of those windows. We were all so young, so full of promise, of ambition, of good intentions of making the world a better place. I was elected by the largest majority possible by Gray's Inn to the senate of the Bar Council and suffered the frustration that every young person must find when what seem to them their bright solutions to every problem are regarded by their older and wiser mentors with the polite disdain that they deserve. One of the worst abuses of young barristers in my day was that solicitors sat on their fees and didn't pay them over. There was one firm of solicitors, which no longer exists, based in expensive premises, who boasted that they paid their rent on the interest earned on counsel's fees that they'd deposited. I came up with what I thought was the brilliant idea of making it mandatory on all barristers to report any such solicitor to the Bar Council if they hadn't paid the fees after six months. I still think it's a good idea but it was knocked to the boundary with great ease by the high heid yins. When you're young, or it was certainly so in my day, everything's so black and white and everything is so important.

One of my great joys about Gray's Inn was dining in Hall. The Bar was a very small profession, and the Inns of Court smaller still and you were obliged to eat thirty-six dinners before you could be called to the Bar (only three a term would be counted but you could eat there as often as you liked). It's actually a very sensible idea as in rural communities, where everybody knows everybody, you are able to assess people's reliability or lack of it, and so it was in your Inn, where you would meet the barristers, the benchers (the governing body of the Inn), you would hold debates and 'Moots', which are a form of mock trial, in front of the benchers in Hall so that by the time you came to be called they had a fairly good estimate of your abilities and indeed your worth. I'm not here referring to financial worth; that has never been a matter of much concern within the practice of the Bar. The system allows the young and intelligent to make their way up the scale and perhaps to earn quite substantial amounts of money.

I once debated with the actor Robert Morley as guest speaker on the motion, 'This house would plough up the playing fields of Eton and give the produce to the poor.' Robert Morley had chosen the topic himself and I assumed it was to be a debate about private and public education, but in fact Morley's choice was because he actually hated team games and it was only the playing fields that he wanted to dig up. It turned into a very jolly evening. In the course of my research I discovered that the great names of the golden age of the Bar, Lord Birkett, Sir Edward Marshall Hall, F.E. Smith and of course at that time our own Lord Denning, were not the products of public school education, but had all risen through the grammar school system (although Marshall Hall did spend one year at Rugby). And Norman Birkett boasted that he had learned the art of jury speeches while selling cottons and needles to the ladies in his father's haberdashery shop. F.E. Smith's mother was a cleaning lady, while Marshall Hall's parents were itinerant actors who were forever floating ahead of the bailiffs but, in his case, took their child with them. One is reminded that Tony Blair's grandparents were from a similar background and left their son behind in the keeping of the people who ran the theatrical lodgings, Mr and Mrs Blair, who adopted him.

Certainly the traditions of my Inn of Court were designed to get people up on their feet and trying out their embryonic speaking skills. One of the more delightful methods of doing this was the system of fines. The senior barrister in Hall would be called upon to adjudicate on alleged breaches of regulations, brought by one young barrister or student against another, or against the whole mess, and they could be very witty and amusing charges. If the fine was awarded it was a bottle of port at a highly subsidised rate and if it failed, the failed applicant had to buy a bottle of port for the mess. This practice has now ceased in this politically correct world, I think on the basis that people might feel bullied or harassed. I'm slightly at a loss to understand what sort of world the Inn thinks it's sending its students out into.

In any event this was a part of my life that I never thought would be restored to me, a piece of the jigsaw that would be for ever lost under the sofa. But I had reckoned without my friends. I've always been blessed by my friends; my family is another matter but my friends can't be faulted. And one of these friends is Libby Watkins née Arfon-Jones, who was one of the people who lived in the family home in Circus Road with me after my mother's death. Libby is very Welsh and effervescent and enormously good fun. Sometimes her parents, AJ and Margaret, would come up and stay as well. Margaret had been at school with Labour Prime Minister Harold Wilson's wife Mary and also wrote poetry.

I owe Brian, Libby's elegant husband, a deep apology because in *Spilling the Beans* I erroneously said that he was ambassador of Ghana, whereas he was in fact ambassador of the fairly newly formed Kingdom of Swaziland and has wonderful stories to tell about their times out there. The King of Swaziland is a polygamist, in that he has many wives and this gave Libby the opportunity to come out with the beautiful line: 'I couldn't possibly come between a man and his wives.' When they had finished their diplomatic roaming, they returned to their native Wales, living in Chepstow. Brian became High Sheriff of the county and Libby went back to the practice of law and became very high-powered indeed in that section of the judiciary that deals with appeals concerning immigration.

Libby is a woman of enormous determination, a Welsh terrier when engaged in a tussle, and she decided that I should be restored to my Inn of Court. Personally I didn't hold up much hope about this. After all, Gray's Inn had, when Optomen had requested to film *Two Fat Ladies* there, declined on the basis that it wasn't suitable and we had gone on to film at Lincoln's Inn. But Libby is nothing if not persistent and finally last year's treasurer, Michael Beloff QC, suggested that she bring me to their annual garden party to see what the reaction was. Unfortunately it coincided with a game fair I was committed to attend so I was unable to go.

She was joined in her campaign by another very tenacious friend of hers, Penny Hamilton. Penny had always been much involved in the life of the Inn, helping write reviews and nobody who ever heard her sing 'The Streets of London' in Gray's Inn Hall will forget it; she has the most splendid voice. Penny was very good to me at the beginning of my drinking and she read at my mother's funeral. She and her husband Nick generously had me to stay in their house as my drinking escalated, and they came with me on the trip to Antigua when I chartered a yacht, *Good Hope*. I'm still the proud possessor of pictures of myself with the three-legged dog that adopted me when we visited the island of St Vincent; one of the photos is particularly remarkable because the dog is standing on two of its legs, so that it can scratch with the third. I had lost touch with them in the early eighties after the death of my dear Clive, when I spiralled even more out of control, a shameful thing to do, particularly as I had just been made godmother to their eldest son, Henry.

With both Libby and Penny on the case, the future looked bright indeed and on their advice I wrote to the incoming treasurer, Sir Mark Waller, asking whether I might be re-admitted to the Inn. The matter went before Pension, which is the meeting of the benchers of the Inn, and I received a letter telling me that I would be welcome.

I had assured Sir Mark that it was not my intention to return to practice; as I said to him, I'm a far better cook than ever I was a barrister, and so it was that I was invited to speak at a mixed mess night in Gray's Inn Hall. This is an occasion where benchers, barristers and students all dine together. Although, strictly speaking the date falls outside the remit of this book, for the sake of completeness I must finish the story. The day of this dinner was also the day of President Barack Obama's inauguration in the United States, so I was able to begin my address with the words that it was a great day for camels going through the eyes of needles, as not very long ago nobody would have thought that either event were possible. I sat on the top table, the benchers table, between Mark Waller and my dear friend Professor David Casson and did my very best not to cry.

A great many people had come quite a long way to attend: among them my friend Debbie, who was once confronted by a misogynistic divorce tutor in a lecture asking her what her grounds for divorce would be if she had been married to another student and he left her bed for a female gorilla. She looked at him rather blankly and he said, 'Bestiality! Bestiality!' To which she replied to great cheers, 'But, Commander Padley, surely it would be insanity?' There were friends from the past and from my chambers who were now senior judges. One of them reminded me of an occasion when I had chased him down Inner Temple Lane, brandishing the swordstick that lived in my umbrella and threatening to kill him. In great fear and trepidation he'd had to go and hide behind the Lord Chancellor of the day who was processing up the lane. Another bencher recalled when the brief of a rather irascible member of our chambers had been filled with confetti and stapled shut so that when he rose to his feet, he was forced to rip it open and confetti flew everywhere around the court. The students present looked on aghast. It is, as I said, a much more respectable age than ours was, but I live in hope that they may take a little inspiration from us. One friend had even flown over from Guernsey simply to be there and I think was giving me two of the ninety days that tax exiles are allowed to spend in this country.

It was very difficult not to cry with the pure emotion of it. Penny pointed out that there were now no sugar lumps on the table which was probably due to the fact that I used to be able to bounce a sugar lump from one wall to the other and up into the gallery. The screen of the gallery came from the poop deck of a Spanish Armada galleon. Gray's Inn was very much the Tudor Inn; pictures of Francis Bacon and Walsingham and the Cecils and all the other Tudor and early Jacobean dignitaries adorn the walls and in a safe somewhere is a confits box that was given to the Inn by St Edmund Campion, who was at that time not yet a Jesuit priest and subsequent martyr but a bright young man, beloved of Elizabeth I. The Walks in Gray's Inn were home to very old catalpa trees which were planted by Francis Bacon when he was treasurer from seeds and seedlings brought back from the first colony in Virginia. And it is supposed to be in Gray's Inn Walks that Francis Bacon unfortunately caught pneumonia while stuffing a dead chicken with snow to see if it would preserve it and died as a result.

Afterwards I had the opportunity to mingle with the other students and young barristers and one very dashing young man came up to me and said, 'I believe you were at my parents' wedding,' and indeed I was. They were married in Llanelli, with two small page boys wearing Llanelli rugby kit if my memory serves me right, and most of us went down for the event. I remember that afterwards we went to the Indian restaurant in Llanelli which oddly didn't serve rice at all. It had every curry you could think of but it only served them with chips. We were all still in our wedding finery and got some very strange looks from the inhabitants of the town. Later, while we were finishing our dinner, a punch-up broke out over a rugby score in the main square and it was with great difficulty that I was persuaded not to go and join in. I gave this young man a great hug and told him the story of how his mother had once appeared in front of a judge who had asked her why she wasn't at home washing the dishes, to which she had given the quick riposte, 'May it please your honour, I have a dishwashing machine.' Both his parents are now fairly senior circuit judges.

I went back to the Goring Hotel with Libby and David Casson, enclosed in yet another golden bubble after the most magical of evenings. I only hope now that I am restored to the bosom of the Inn that there are things I can do that may be of some use, to make amends for my misbehaviour in days gone by. This summer will see the first Gray's Inn Ball in the Walks, and I've already offered my services to Penny who is on the committee. And croquet is back in the Walks. I used to spend long, happy summer days playing croquet there and it will be nice to do so again, especially now I have my eyes restored. It is wonderful to be back and I hope that perhaps after my years in the wilderness and my experiences in Alcoholics Anonymous I can proffer some useful advice with regard to the huge numbers of criminals who are afflicted with alcoholism and other addictions. Not to be kind and to pamper them, because that is not the way to persuade people to get sober, but simply to understand the illness in its entirety and look at different ways of handling it.

Do I regret that I'm not a member of the legal profession? Probably not. I am, after all, what I am. My path has been a different one from theirs; it's not the path that in my twenties I thought I would ever follow. In fact it would have to be a very bizarre thought process indeed that would take me through my life as it has been, and now here I am, at sixty-one, cook, Fat Lady, countryside campaigner, and I think I'm quite happy with the strangeness of my lot.

I didn't sleep very much that night, partly from joy and partly from thinking of ghosts. The Bar has a high mortality rate. The stresses and strains, the irregular hours and meals and travelling and staying in strange places all take their toll. Those colleagues didn't live long enough to achieve their potential, but they all came into my mind's eye that night. I miss them all and it just makes me grateful that I and so many others have survived. As Mark Waller put it, very charmingly I thought, in the 1980s the wheels came off my bike. Boy, did they ever. I was always the one most unlikely to survive.

Stuffed Sprats

For me as a London child, the Lord Mayor's Show on the Saturday before Armistice Sunday was a great highlight of the year. The Lord Mayor's Show coincides with the run of sprats up the River Thames and traditionally sprats are always eaten at the Lord Mayor's inaugural banquet. This is a dish we used to have at home as a supper dish or a lunch dish with hot crusty bread. It's sprats with anchovies.

2lb (900g) sprats
2oz (50g) tinned anchovy fillets
2oz (50g) white breadcrumbs
salt and pepper
2oz (50g) butter
some lemons

Preheat the oven to 180°C/350°F/gas mark 4. Gut your sprats and remove the backbone. If you are squeamish, take the heads off, otherwise, leave them on. Roll the sprats round a piece of anchovy and place the roll in a buttered fireproof dish. Sprinkle the whole with breadcrumbs, season with salt and pepper and dot with butter. Bake in the oven for 15 to 20 minutes and serve with lemon quarters. It's a very good and comforting dish.

December

The north wind doth blow and we will have snow,
And what will the robin do then, poor thing?
He'll sit in the barn and keep himself warm
And hide his head under his wing, poor thing,
And so should you!

And so I drove home via Cheshire for a couple of speaking engagements. The last one of the year was the Cheshire Forest Hunt and they gave me a large hamper of food, Sally Aspen, the Hunt Supporters secretary, filling it with all sorts of things that I like, such as venison kidneys. I've always said that the day they hang me I will have roe deer kidneys for breakfast, but all venison kidneys are good. The great advantage of your last meal, of course, is that you don't have to worry about indigestion so that whenever people ask me, the menu seems to get longer and longer so it will be a long night. Another delicacy in the hamper were quail's eggs which, astonishingly, had come from a quail that her daughter had hatched from a supermarket box of quail's eggs. You read of this from time to time, especially quail and duck eggs being hatched in an incubator from supermarket eggs and this somewhat perplexes me because, as far as I'm aware, poultry don't actually need the presence of a cockerel in order to lay eggs, so why are supermarkets selling impregnated eggs?

I'm always fascinated by how many people in urban surroundings keep chickens. My own nephew, Edward, had chickens in his garden in Balham and one of them would actually come and sit on the old laundry hoist in the kitchen. Where I live, the children used to have bantams, charming little things that ran around shrieking and could ruin my garden.

They used to come and peck at the downstairs window of the manor house for food, or get into the front hall and perch on the umbrella stands. The cockerel used to go in downstairs and sleep on top of the bookcase, which gave my neighbour Charlie Fletcher, the children's author, the opportunity to say, in the middle of an incredibly boring meeting, 'Oh look, my cock's gone to sleep.' As none of the other people in the meeting were aware of the presence of the bantam cockerel, it caused great consternation and no doubt livened up the meeting enormously. I love the unusualness of people, don't you?

I have a friend in Cheshire who is a slightly eccentric country lady who knew about her broad beans or the problems of dealing with slugs and I only discovered the other day, having known her for years, that she cooked for the Beatles at their Apple offices for a whole year. She said that she and her friend answered the advertisement and went for the interview in their twin-sets and pearls and tweed skirts, not terribly sure who they were supposed to be going to cook for, which is probably the reason they got the job. She said it was all very peculiar. John Lennon, who was on a macrobiotic regime, ate brown rice but with beluga caviar. George Harrison ate one-egg omelettes and Ringo Starr had a tomato soup recipe that he insisted was all he was going to eat. She was there when the Beatles sang on the roof and she said that all the great and the good of the musical world walked through her kitchen pretty much on a daily basis.

Cooking is a great skill to have, and one that is too often underestimated. There are endless jobs to be found all over the world and with interesting people, which aren't necessarily all that complicated. I know one girl who, while she was an incredibly good cook, got a job paying a ridiculously high sum of money simply to serve hamburgers and soup to a houseful of whores in a smart ski resort. An Arab sheik had brought them and kept them there for his delectation and would send cars for them at all hours of the day and night.

Joanna Lumley's activities on behalf of the Gurkhas, seeking the right for Gurkhas who retired from the army before 1997 to live in the UK and to get a pension, and quite right too, reminded me of the time Jennifer and I went to cook for them, and they were delightful: small, smiley, laughing men, and masters of camouflage. Two of them in camouflage rig literally fell down in front of us and the camera, and although we knew where they were we simply couldn't see them despite their being only a few yards away from us. They cooked us curry and we cooked a dinner for the officers' mess. We also ate their army rations with them which come in strange foil bags that you heat up in a pan full of water, and which were actually not half bad. Better than a lot of the food I get served at some of the functions I attend. Yet the Gurkhas are probably the world's most lethal killers. One of the officers told me that they each have a working khukuri, their traditional large curved knife, and a ceremonial one but they also have, hidden away, another khukuri which is a family knife they have inherited from their fathers and grandfathers and is the one they use for taking heads. It is razor-sharp, and never drawn without shedding blood, even if it's only their own because they will nick their thumb when cleaning it so that it tastes blood on every occasion that it's drawn. Their commanding officer, who was the first Gurkha colonel of infantry – up until then the colonels had always been British officers – was the most extraordinary man. It was like being in a room with a caged tiger, he exuded so much energy and tension. I remember the sound man shouting, 'Quiet please.' I thought the colonel was going to take his head, he was so angry to be shouted at in his own quarters and I had great difficulty explaining to him that the sound man just shouted at random to everybody before a take.

December is the month I spend at home. Home to mountains of post, cups of coffee with the media, cups of tea over at the main house, seeing my friends in the village, going to Valvona and Crolla to eat truffles and pasta and strachiatelli soup, and just generally wind down. As you might imagine, having read this book, I am by this time of the year pretty exhausted. I vowed that next year I'm not going to run around so much, so please don't invite me to come to your events because I find it awfully difficult to say no to you, but I'm really getting too old for this and must get more rest. My friend Carin, who came from Spain to see me for Christmas, didn't get the cosiest reception in the world because all I wanted to do was collapse in a heap. It is a time to watch rugby, to turn off, to read books and think about the food for Christmas. Everybody gets in a terrible state about food at Christmas, but actually it's the easiest meal in the world because its components are fixed. I get phone calls from friends asking me how to cook a goose or how to make oyster stuffing or when one should make Christmas pudding. Well, if you're asking about pudding in December, it's too late because you should have made it at Stir-up Sunday earlier in the year, Stir-up Sunday being in October.

One of the disadvantages of my new television is that I occasionally watch cooking programmes and was horrified to hear Simon Rimmer say, when somebody asked about Stir-up Sunday, 'Oh, that's old-fashioned stuff, we don't do that any more.' I generally try to avoid watching cookery programmes, partly because most of them aren't terribly good and I don't much like the food, but I suppose there is a certain seed of bitterness in my heart that other people are making them and not me. But then, just when I feel that I've lived too long and am too out of kilter with the world, something happens that shows that the pendulum has shifted and cheers me up enormously.

I found myself nominated and indeed short-listed as a 'Rural Hero', in a new category in the Countryside Alliance award scheme. I've long been an admirer of the way that these Countryside Alliance awards have grown. They started with 'Best Raw Producer' then had 'Best Post Office', then 'Best Village Shop' and they really do celebrate the little people who are fighting hard against bureaucratic barriers in order to serve the local community, to serve local foods and local farmers in a way that nobody else does. I decided that having been short-listed in December, I had better go to the awards, which took place in March 2009 so I'm taking a leap forward beyond my year to tell you about it.

The other people on the short-list included Ian Pigott, who I rather hoped would win. He was a delightful young man who started Farm Sunday which is an enormously good link between towns and countryside and saw in its first year 400 farms opening to the public to encourage people to take their children to see the animals and teach them how farms work. It was, I think, a hugely successful venture which I hope will grow and grow. I was slightly surprised to find journalist Janet Street-Porter on the short-list since she has never struck me as somebody with any sort of rural interest, although she is of course a rambler and presumably was nominated by the Ramblers Association. Ramblers are a breed apart from the countryside and tend not to be in favour of most country practices and particularly field sports. Her nomination was because of her support for British veal on Gordon Ramsay's food programme, *The F Word*. The countryside needs any help it can get and so I was pleased to see her name on the list.

My sister Heather used to produce the most delicious dish of loin of veal, boned and stuffed with its own kidneys and cooked on a bed of onions with red wine. You'll find the recipe in *Clarissa's Comfort Food*. I'm not a huge fan of veal, despite the fact that my own butcher, Colin Peat, is one of the few in Scotland who does sell it. But clearly if you're going to have a dairy industry, you have to have veal, otherwise there would be no milk or cheese because it would all have gone to calves that aren't necessarily the right breed to make the best beef. And so the beef calves need to be knocked on the head and the best thing to do in those circumstances is to eat them, which is always the best answer where food is concerned when there is a surplus.

Beef calves remind me of Carla Lane, the animal activist who objected to the practice of crating veal calves so that the meat is white. Some years later a number of farmers took their bull calves and dumped them on Carla Lane, who seemed to have forgotten that animals grow up, because she found herself appealing for funds as she was running out of money to look after thirty fully grown bulls. Bulls are not easy to keep nor are they friendly animals and of course Health and Safety were complaining, not only about the bulls' living conditions but also about the danger they posed to other people.

I suppose what makes me so cross, both about the antis and about the fluffy bunny brigade alike is their lack of common sense, their lack of thinking things through. Country people live with life and death and animals and their ways from birth and understand the turning of the seasons and the fact that they are producing food for the nation, no matter how fond they become of their animals. Whereas urban people don't like to think of the connection between animals and the meat they eat. They don't allow that people in the country perhaps know what they're doing and have done it for centuries. As one old gamekeeper said to me when we were filming *Clarissa and the Countryman*, 'Tell them people in the towns that when they sort out their own problems then perhaps they can come and talk to us.'

Thus I found myself at the Cholmondeley Room of the House of Lords on a rather beautiful day so that the windows were open on to the river, and I have to say that the award ceremony was pleasingly swift. We were served finger food which was perfectly all right and I saw lots of old friends, among them Benji Mancroft who was standing beside me eyeing up the cormorants on the river; always a delight to see him. He's the most beautifully and immaculately dressed man that you could ever hope to find and has a wicked sense of humour so that would have made it a pleasure from the start. In any event I did not win the Rural Hero award, which went, as I'd hoped, to Ian Pigott. The only thing I envied him was the rather attractive plate decorated with ducks that was his reward.

The real pleasure, however, came afterwards, when I got the opportunity to meet the various producers who were on the short-list. I was particularly pleased to see Peter Greig from Pipers Farms in Devon because he and his wife and I were right there campaigning with Henrietta Green's army in the days of her food fairs and the opening of Borough Market. Pipers Farms is a very clever idea whereby all the farms and the producers in a particular valley in Devon have got together to sell their produce almost as a commune. It was they who first reminded me, some fifteen years ago now, how much chicken production had deteriorated when they sold me a breast of chicken stuffed with apricots and said you have to cook it for x amount of time and I said, 'Surely not, isn't that too long?' They said, 'Clarissa, have you forgotten how long you used to have to cook a chicken for?' And they were of course quite right. These modern, rubbishy things that are raised in five weeks from egg to table fall apart if you keep them in the oven for more than about forty-five minutes.

We reminisced about the amount of groundwork we had done to promote the idea of the small food producer and the quality of their produce. It is so difficult to believe how little there was back in 1987 and how really it was only Henrietta Green who was walking the walk for the small producer, and how far we've come since then. Peter Greig was talking to me about the Slow Food movement and how they've become involved in that. This started in Italy some years ago and has grown like Topsy and is really not so much about cooking your food slowly as growing and rearing it slowly with care and love and attention. It is a great organisation. And he told me that Michael Caines, who is the chef now at Gidleigh Park in Devon, has been doing a lot to try to unite Devon and Tuscany. It seems an unlikely combination to me but I expect he knows what he's doing. It was lovely to see Peter and his wife again and to remember how far we have come and he said, and I think quite rightly, that the work we did back then is here to stay and is not going to come undone now, so we just have to build on it and keep up the quality.

A lot of people wanted to come and have their picture taken with me or talk to me; one of them was a most delightful butcher from Doddington in Kent, there with his family, one of the few butchers who still have their own slaughterhouse and he said, 'Would you ever come and see me?' My friend Olga Romanoff lives just down the road from him at Faversham and it emerged that she was one of their customers; they said that they were looking to have a 'By Appointment to the House of Romanoff' sign over their shop (her father was the son of Tsar Nicholas II's sister), but it hadn't happened yet.

One of the most impressive pieces of paper I was handed was the menu from the Feathers Inn in Hedley on the Hill in Northumberland who were Yorkshire and North-East Pub of the Year in 2008 and Local Food Pub of the Year in 2008 as well, which doesn't surprise me in the least. The menu I was given was for 7 February and was full of just the sort of dishes I would like to eat. Among the starters there was potted local hare; air-dried ham with celeriac coleslaw on toast; home-made black pudding with poached egg and devilled gravy; and even cold roast rib of beef from Haden Bridge, aged for twenty-eight days. What was particularly impressive about this menu was the back of it, which had a map of Northumberland, including the site of the pub and listing all the local farms from which they sourced their ingredients. There were nineteen of those in total and they varied from pedigree Longhorn beef to a butcher selling locally sourced meat, through Highland cattle, Dexter cattle and butchers sourcing local lamb and pork as well. Their oysters came from Lindisfarne, which I have visited twice. The first trip was when I was staying at Spittal and just went across to see what it was all about. And I'd just come up from Topsham in Devon where people were getting terribly excited because they'd spotted a couple of avocets, and on the causeway out to Lindisfarne there were so many avocets they were trying to get into the car with me. My second visit was with Johnny when we were filming *Clarissa and the Countryman*. We had wanted to film with the oyster producers but for some reason, I can't remember why, it wasn't feasible. I think it might have been because it was the foot and mouth era and all sorts of restrictions were in force.

The Feathers Inn menu even listed their egg supplier, their vegetable supplier, their supplier of cheeses, milk and cream and, much to my surprise, chillies from somebody in Haltwhistle. For those of you who don't know it, Haltwhistle is actually the centre of the British Isles, up on the old Roman military road that runs parallel with the A69 across from Newcastle to Carlisle. The pub even has pedigree Jersey ice cream from somebody in Stocksfield. I must go and see them the next time I'm up. It was a cleverly thought-out menu but also one that delighted my heart because I've now lived in the north for fifteen years and it's not easy, or it certainly wasn't when I first moved up, to find proper suppliers in Northumberland.

I found myself with a card from a pub called the Gaggle of Geese in Buckland Newton near Dorchester. My only visit to the Piddle Valley was for somebody's wedding many years ago when I was still at Gray's Inn and we went and stayed in this tiny little pub called the Brace of Pheasants at Plush. It was then that I discovered that Pid was the Celtic god of rain and is the origin of such words as piddle and puddle and so forth and in fact the Long Man of Wilmington, that strange chalk cutting near Eastborne, is supposedly Pid opening the gates of rain which is why, unlike the Cerne Abbas giant, he's not flashing his willy, because he has his back to you. We were told that it was still regarded as a fertility site by the country women around Wilmington and people used to go up there in the middle of the night and leave their knickers as a trophy to Pid in the hope that they might produce a baby.

I had a slightly ridiculous conversation with Newlyns Farm Shop which turns out to be in an area of Hampshire through which I travel with monotonous regularity. I got it into my head for some reason that they were from Newlyn in Cornwall and they looked rather mystified as to why I told them that I was going to Cornwall in the autumn. Apart from having the most fantastic farm shop selling all varieties of local produce, they also have a café and run a cookery school, offering demonstrations for ladies who lunch, through to pâtés, pies and terrines, down to Indian or French cuisine and knife skills and butchery. But what particularly impressed me about it was the fact that they ran courses for both children and teenagers. The children's courses were run for eight- to twelve-year-olds and, as they said, weren't really great money-makers as they were very labour-intensive but they were interested in getting the younger generation to learn about food and where it comes from. I mean, so many children in this country think food just comes in packets from supermarkets and don't in any way link it with the animals or the soil or anything else. The teenagers' courses go from thirteen years old upwards, and on both courses I noticed that in December they do a Christmas presents course which I think is an excellent idea because all too often children simply don't know what to give.

One of the best documents I was given at this event was the map of the Ribble Valley Food Trail. The Ribble Valley is that area of the British Isles where the Queen would most like to retire to and raise horses. Fat chance, I should think. The Ribble Valley runs through Lancashire, through Clitheroe, and up towards Yorkshire, and the local council has very cleverly produced a map with a food trail that shows you not only local pubs and eateries along the way but lists all the local suppliers, presumably for tourists who are staying in the Lake District, to say nothing of the people who actually live in that part of the world, such as cheese shops and fisheries and producers of organic flour. There's one particularly charming picture of a butcher's in Chipping, near Preston, called Robinson Brothers, which shows a picture of one of the family walking with his crook through a very attractive-looking flock of sheep.

Because the M65 is so frequently blocked with traffic, the roads north of it, the A677 or the A680, are roads that I travel quite often, driving from Cheshire across to Yorkshire and now I shall take this map with me and be able to make detours on what looks like a really interesting set of explorations. I imagine that if you go on to the website for ribblevalleyfoodtrail.co.uk you'll be able to download this particular map for yourself and explore should you find yourself in that part of the world. It is so nice to find a local council investing in food producers in this way and also to have access to so many suppliers. Most councils do nothing but cause problems in my experience. When Henrietta wrote *British Food Finds* and then her *Food Lovers' Guide to Britain* one could travel round the country stopping off at various producers and buying delicious foods to take home. Henrietta would tramp the roads with her Yorkshire terrier, Violet, who was I think one of the most unpleasant dogs I ever met, but much beloved by Henrietta, and cross-examine producers exhaustively before they made it into her *Food Lovers' Guide*. Sadly that book went out of print and I never felt that *Rick Stein's Food Heroes* had the same level of personal knowledge.

With all my travels, I wonder if I will ever manage to stay home long enough to hang my pictures, of which I have many. Not particularly valuable ones but pictures that I like. One is by

Lionel Edwards entitled *Every Dog Has His Day* which portrays the Waterloo Cup with the bank in the background and the judge on his horse, and a mongrel, a mutt of sorts, has got loose from the crowd, trailing his lead, and he's come through between two very well-bred greyhounds and grabbed the hare as the greyhounds look on in astonishment. It's a picture I've tried to find for years and years and Lindsey Knapp of the Victoria Gallery finally managed to find it for me. On previous occasions she's found me the wrong picture, which is also entitled *Every Dog Has His Day* and is by Cecil Aldin and shows a huntsman and well-bred hounds looking on in amazement at this cocky terrier that is walking through, carrying a large, ugly-looking rat that it's killed. It takes time to hang pictures; not the physical act of hanging them but deciding where you're going to put them and what goes best where and will be seen to best advantage. It's a task that I really need to make the time to do.

I also need to find time to cook, to invent new recipes. As I stand at the moment, I don't think I'd be able to produce another recipe book because I've now written fifteen books of which eight are cookery books and that is a lot of recipes, recipes of my life. I really should spend time thinking of fresh ideas and flavours and original ways to do things.

On the day that I write this there is news that Warwickshire police have arrested two men for the murder of a hunt follower, Trevor Morse. The two men in question had been following the hunt in a gyrocopter, which is a sort of small helicopter, and monitoring what the hunt was doing for some weeks and the Warwickshire Hunt had been sufficiently worried about their presence to alert the Civil Aviation Authority and the police, but nothing was done and they were allowed to continue. It is still more alarming to note that the probable reason why the antis were pursuing the Warwickshire Hunt was that Otis Ferry, precluded from visiting his own hounds until that day, had actually been hunting with the Warwickshire earlier that week. Now they have killed somebody in the hunting community, and ignoring the question of whether it was murder or not, the fact remains that a man is dead, and his death was the result of their actions. For what? So that they could disrupt an activity which, at worst, if the Warwickshire were breaching the Hunting Act, would only have resulted in the death of a fox. Curiously, I'm reminded that in Gibbon's *Decline and Fall of the Roman Empire*, talking about the last days of the Empire, he said that 'At such time, men turn to vegetarian diets and set up animals as Gods.' So nothing ever changes it would seem.

I met a rather good man today, Professor Philip Hanlon, who is Professor of Public Health at Glasgow University. We were appearing together on BBC Radio Scotland to discuss food in these times and the horrendous increase in the buying of junk food because people have less money. In the course of the programme he said that it might be a lot sooner than people actually thought that we would need to be growing all our own food and not importing it. He also told me the rather interesting fact that not one single ingredient in Walkers shortbread is grown or produced in Scotland, a terrifying admission when you think that Jenners, now owned by the House of Fraser and once the high point of Edinburgh shopping, sells a pallet-load of Walkers shortbread every week. So if you're a farmer or a food producer, hang on in there because by dint of circumstances and this curious hike in food prices and collapse in money, the whole situation in world food production is about to change. They have a saying in AA which is, 'Don't quit before the miracle happens.'

Talking of miracles turns my mind to religion and one of my stranger fundraising exercises which was to help to save St Woolos Cathedral, an enchanting little Norman cathedral in Newport in Monmouthshire. I had been introduced to the dean by my friend Libby at the Athenaeum – it was all rather out of Trollope – but he was the most delightful man by the name of Richard Fenwick who persuaded me that what I wanted to do was go and give a talk to raise money for the restoration fund for St Woolos Cathedral. St Woolos, I should tell you, was a sixth-century pirate who preyed on shipping along the Welsh coast until he married a good woman and was converted to Christianity and in the fullness of time became a saint. What he actually did to become a saint isn't quite clear. There are a lot of saints like that in the British hierarchy. If you go to Cornwall, they have more saints there than anywhere else in the British Isles, the reason being that when the Christian Church was attempting to gain a foothold in Cornwall, the ruling house pointed out that when they died under the terms of their then religion they automatically became demi-gods and so a deal was cut that they would become saints instead.

It was dark when I arrived in Newport, which is a maze of one-way streets and poor signage and finally in despair I stopped at the only premises that appeared to be open in the street and I found myself in a betting shop. An Irishman came forward to greet me and I asked him if he knew the way to St Woolos Cathedral, rather expecting him to say that he was a stranger there. He said, 'Oh come on, I've finished now, I'll come and show you the way.' I must have looked slightly apprehensive at the thought of getting into my car with a total stranger because he said, 'Sure, haven't I seen you at Bandon?' Bandon is a town in West Cork, where the Somerville and Ross novels are set, and the Clonakilty hounds are still kennelled in the middle of the town and you hear their music in the morning. There is only one reason I have ever been to Bandon and that is for coursing, to an invitation stakes we go over for every year which is held on the farm of a most delightful man who has an old donkey tethered outside. When I asked him about the donkey he said, 'Sure, every time I was in trouble, wasn't the donkey there with me?' So I shook the hand of this mysterious Irishman and we climbed into my car and under his direction drove all the way up to the top of the town to the cathedral.

It was raining and he didn't have a coat so I asked if he would be all right and he said that his sister lived in that part of the town and he'd go and have a cup of tea with her. I was amazed at how charming and how selflessly helpful he had been, and it would clearly have been an insult to offer him money. I was sitting in my car musing on this when my mobile phone rang and it was Richard saying, 'Where are you?' I told him I was right outside and I went in and had a bowl of soup with him before we went off to the university campus where the talk was being held. After my experience at Ely, where I was sitting under the octagon, talking to the assembled crowd, I had rather hoped it might have taken place in the cathedral, but that was not to be.

Richard, who is full of the joys of life, showed me into his study and said, 'Come and see our vices,' and there was a large organ and two Welsh harps. The harps were played by his wife, while he was an expert on the organ. Afterwards I stayed with Libby and Brian in Chepstow and we had a dinner party the following night which was indeed straight out of Trollope as there were three clergy among the guests.

And so finally it was Christmas and it was time to cook the goose and the Christmas ham and the most exquisite Christmas beef which had been hung for eight weeks and just generally relax at home. I spent my winnings on Wales beating Australia at rugby on beluga caviar; I thought this seemed a suitable use for such a windfall, then I thought rather better of John Lennon than I had ever done before but I still passed on the brown rice.

So there you have it, a conglomerate year in the life of Clarissa. By the time this is published we will not be far away from the next general election, so please, please let's get rid of these horrendous New Labour politicians who have so wrecked our country over the last twelve years. I will say one thing for Teflon Tony, he's about the only politician I know of who had the sense to get out while the going was good. You might say 'one jump ahead of the hangman', unlike Baroness Thatcher who I sometimes see bumbling around lost in a complete world of her own which is probably the best place for her. Anyway, remember that when the Conservatives last left power the economy was thriving, thanks to Ken Clark, and we were in a solid position; you know where we are today. If there is to be any hope for the country and the countryside, we really do need a Conservative government and I'd remind you this comes from someone who once chaired the Liberal Party eve-of-election conference in Scotland.

I hope you have enjoyed this book and that it's given you things to think about. I've rifled through a lot of drawers to put it together. At the suggestion of my dear agent, Heather Holden-Brown, I have given some saws, or sayings, at the beginning of each of the months of the year. This came about because of the snow at the beginning of 2009 when she was remarking how cold it was, there having been a mild spell before, and I came out with, 'Don't cast a clout till May is out.' And she said, 'Oh yes, that's good, you should have some saws.' I'm still not sure whether that particular one refers to the May flower or the month of May but in any event, now that I've persuaded you to wear wool perhaps you should do away with the central heating, and you might like to think of wearing a vest as well. I hope you like the recipes too. It might seem rather strange for you to find them but I would like to point out that some of my drawers contain recipes and there is an old tradition of putting recipes in unlikely places. There's a book called *Sea* which is a novel that has recipes at the end of every chapter and I once read a truly dreadful book by Fanny Cradock called *The Lormes of Castle Rising* whose only claim to fame was that at various stages throughout the book she gave recipes so you'd have, 'William the Conqueror came and dined at the castle on Tripes à la mode de Caen*', the asterisk sending you to the bottom of the page and a recipe for that dish. The recipes were the best part of the book by far and I hope you won't say that about this book, but that you enjoy them nonetheless.

I shall no doubt see you at a game fair or at the side of a field somewhere in the years ahead, if the antis don't manage to kill me at my forthcoming court case. I must remember to ring up the Chief Constable of North Yorkshire and ask him how he intends to protect me, since when we were filming *Clarissa and the Countryman* I was once warned away from filming at Stroud's farmers' market because the police said that they could not guarantee our safety. While I'm sure there are plenty of muscular countrymen who would volunteer to come to Scarborough with me to guard my back, I would not like to put them at risk of being falsely accused of some nefarious crime by the antis. I have great faith in British justice so I hope that I shall be acquitted but if for some reason I'm not, I leave you with the thought that the last relatives I had who were tried in Yorkshire were hung, drawn and quartered with Guy Fawkes so, whatever happens, the outcome has to be better than that. Maybe I should just volunteer to do community service and follow in Jamie Oliver's footsteps, teaching the young of Yorkshire to cook. It is highly unlikely that they would lock me up but I quite fancy the thought of a prison cookbook on how to feed people on seventy-five pence a day. It might be quite a challenge for the credit crisis ahead.

God keep you and bless you all, until we meet again.

Galette des Rois

In the more boisterous days of Christmas, somebody was appointed the King of Mistlerule and that person was chosen because he found the bean in the cake on Christmas Eve. In richer houses it was a gold ring, and in more pious houses it was a symbol of the Christ child. The person who found the object was crowned with a paper crown and was the King of the feast and was able to give everybody directions. It is the forerunner of the coins in the Christmas pudding which Health and Safety now so terribly condemn.

Pastry
9oz (250g) plain flour
½ teaspoon salt
7oz (200g) unsalted butter
1oz (25g) sugar
¼ pint (150ml) approximately of chilled water

Filling
4oz (110g) unsalted butter
4oz (110g) castor sugar
4 egg yolks
a drop of almond essence
1 teaspoon kirsch or something similar
4oz (110g) freshly ground almonds
dried bean or golden ring

For the pastry, sift the flour and the salt in a large bowl, and work into it 3oz (75g) butter together with the sugar until the mixture resembles breadcrumbs. Mix in enough water to make a stiff dough, cover and leave in a cold place or refrigerator for half an hour.

Roll out your pastry to about a quarter of an inch thick. Dot it with a third of the remaining butter. Fold the pastry into three as though you were folding a letter and then do the same in the opposite direction. Cover and refrigerate for half an hour. Repeat the process twice more and leave for another 20 minutes, chilling before using. You can of course go out and buy a packet of puff pastry, but it is nicer if you make it. Divide the pastry in half. Roll each half into a round of about a quarter of an inch thick. Let them rest while you make the filling.

Cream the butter and the sugar together until light and fluffy. Mix in two of the egg yolks, the almond essence, the kirsch and the ground almonds and work together until you have a smooth paste. Place one of your rounds of pastry on a chilled baking tray and then place the filling on top of it, leaving a two-inch border around the margin. Place your object of choice in the mixture. Brush the border with some of the remaining egg yolk. Place the second round of pastry on the top and pinch the edges together tightly and make patterns on the top of the pastry with a knife and paint with the rest of the egg wash. Chill for 45 minutes.

Preheat the oven to 190°C/375°F/gas mark 5 and bake for 20 to 30 minutes until the pastry is crisp and golden.